# LINCOLN UNMASKED

# LINCOLN UNMASKED

## What You're Not Supposed to Know About Dishonest Abe

## Thomas J. DiLorenzo

THREE RIVERS PRESS · NEW YORK

Library of Congress Cataloging-in-Publication Data

DiLorenzo, Thomas J.
Lincoln unmasked : what you're not supposed to know about dishonest Abe /
Thomas J. DiLorenzo.—1st ed.
Includes bibliographical references.
1. Lincoln, Abraham, 1809–1865.   2. Lincoln, Abraham, 1809–1865—Ethics.
3. Lincoln, Abraham, 1809–1865—Public opinion.   4. United States—
Politics and government—1861–1865.   5. Public opinion—United States.
6. Presidents—United States—Biography.   I. Title.
E457 .2.D45 2006
973.7092—dc22        2006012739

ISBN: 978-0-307-33842-6

*Design by Helene Berinsky*

First Paperback Edition

*Dedicated to the memory of*
*Professor Mel Bradford,*
*a gentleman of great learning*
*and intellectual courage.*

# CONTENTS

8          Contents

## PART II
## Economic Issues You're Supposed to Ignore

## PART III
## The Politics of the Lincoln Cult

# LINCOLN UNMASKED

# 1

## Challenging the Gatekeepers

When President Reagan nominated Professor Mel Bradford of the University of Dallas to head the National Endowment for the Humanities in 1981, a group of intellectuals with influence in the administration waged a fierce campaign against the nomination. Their chief complaint was: "He's anti-Lincoln!" Professor Bradford, an expert in the use of rhetoric, had dared to criticize some of Lincoln's deceptive political language in peer-reviewed academic journal articles.[1] Professor Bradford's opponents apparently considered this blasphemous and conducted a vicious political campaign against him. They stooped so low as to spread false rumors that he was a Hitler admirer.[2] Professor Bradford (who passed away in 1993) eventually withdrew his name in disgust. His opponents prevailed; there would be no challenge to the popular view of Abraham Lincoln.

Things have not changed much in the academic world since the Bradford affair. I have been subjected to similar calumny and name-calling, as has anyone else who attempts to deviate from the Official Truth. Lincoln has been portrayed as a saint, and his defenders are so sanctimonious that they consider themselves to be self-appointed Gatekeepers of the Truth. They do whatever is necessary to keep unflattering information about Lincoln from the public. If they do dare to mention such facts, they spin their statements to mislead, misinform, and confuse the reader. One has to wonder: What purpose does all this deception and misinformation serve? If Lincoln was such a saint, why can't his record speak for itself?

The gatekeepers constitute what I call the Lincoln cult. It is mostly composed of academics who have spent their careers carrying on the deification of Abraham Lincoln that began with the New England clergy (and the Republican Party) of the late nineteenth century. As a rule, they ignore unpleasant facts about Lincoln, such as his suspension of habeas corpus, his imprisonment of tens of thousands of Northern political opponents during the War between the States, his shutting down of hundreds of opposition newspapers, his micromanagement of the bombing of Southern cities and the waging of war on civilians, his pledge to support a constitutional amendment prohibiting the federal government from ever interfering with Southern slavery, and his lifelong white supremacist views. If they do mention such things at all, it is only to make voluminous excuses for them or to denounce others who address them in their writing.[3]

According to *Webster's College Dictionary,* a cult is "a group that devotes itself to or venerates a person, ideal, fad, etc." or "a religion or sect considered to be false, unorthodox, or extremist."

The Lincoln cult is interested not so much in research and education about Lincoln and the war—about discovering historical truth—but in maintaining a largely false image of the man whom they call "Father Abraham" and compare to Jesus and Moses. The rest of the academic world engages in vigorous debate and discussion of myriad issues every day; that's what academic freedom is supposed to be all about. But when it comes to the subject of Lincoln, no such debate is permitted by the gatekeepers. There have been heated debates over the legacies of all other presidents, be it Jefferson, Jackson, Wilson, Teddy Roosevelt, FDR, Truman, Reagan, or Clinton, but no such debate is acceptable regarding Lincoln. One has to wonder: What are the gatekeepers afraid of?

The so-called Lincoln scholars' decidedly nonscholarly behavior is motivated primarily by academic self-interest. The academic gatekeepers are paid very well in their academic jobs, and through government and foundation grants as well. They do very well financially on the lecture circuit and use university and foundation funds to give each other "Lincoln Awards" for their scholarship that are sometimes worth tens of thousands of dollars. Any challenges to their views are seen not only as challenges to the Official View of American History, but also to their overblown professional reputations and bank accounts.

Many Lincoln cultists behave in the manner they do because it serves a political agenda as well as a personal one. Left-wing Lincoln cultists run the gamut from mainstream liberals to democratic socialists to hard-core leftists like Eric Foner of Columbia University, who lamented the demise of the Soviet Union. (In a 1991 article in *The Nation* magazine Foner opined that, unlike Mikhail Gorbachev, Lincoln would not have allowed the former Soviet republics to secede peacefully from the Soviet Union.[4]) They are nationalists, like Lincoln, in that they favor a more powerful and more highly centralized (i.e., monopolistic) form of government that can better expand the welfare state, regulate the economy, or adopt socialism.

Right-wing Lincoln cultists such as Harry Jaffa and many of his fellow "Straussians" (followers of the late Leo Strauss of the

University of Chicago) are also nationalists, like Lincoln, because they believe that a more powerful and highly centralized government will serve *their* political agenda of a more aggressive and imperialistic foreign policy. Indeed, in my 2002 debate with Jaffa, sponsored by the Independent Institute of Oakland, California, he declared at one point that 9/11 proved more than ever that "we need a strong central government." It was not just a coincidence that he made this declaration in the context of a debate over Lincoln's legacy.

Thus, one thing that all Lincoln cultists have in common is that they use the Lincoln mythology to advocate a bigger, more centralized, and more interventionist central government for one reason or another.

But the Lincoln "gate" is beginning to rust, which is apparently causing panic among the gatekeepers, who are not at all used to having their ideas challenged. In recent years Charles Adams published *When in the Course of Human Events: Arguing the Case for Southern Secession* and it sold very well, as did my own book, *The Real Lincoln*. Jeffrey Hummel's *Emancipating Slaves, Enslaving Free Men* is another hard-hitting and influential challenge to the Lincoln cult, as is John Remington Graham's *A Constitutional History of Secession*. Professor Clyde Wilson's book *From Union to Empire* contains dozens of brilliant essays that challenge many of the superstitions and half-truths that are the intellectual currency of the Lincoln cult. The 1930s-era classic *Lincoln the Man,* by Edgar Lee Masters, Clarence Darrow's law partner, was recently republished by the Foundation for American Education. (It was the most critical account of Lincoln to be published in the first half of the twentieth century.) *The South Was Right!* by James and Walter Kennedy has sold more than 100,000 copies, according to the authors. *Secession, State, and Liberty,* edited by David Gordon and published by Transaction

Publishers, contains essays by twelve scholars who all write favorably of the right of secession in a free society; most of them excoriate Lincoln for waging the bloodiest war in history just to deny that such a right existed. And Thomas Woods's *New York Times* bestseller, *The Politically Incorrect Guide to American History*, cites many of the preceding authors to arrive at conclusions such as, "States had the right to secede" in 1861; "The War between the States was not launched to free the slaves"; and "Lincoln believed that whites were superior and favored the deportation of freed slaves."

Perhaps even more important is the Internet, which allows scholars to present ideas to the entire world without having to be filtered by gatekeepers of any kind.[5]

*Lincoln Unmasked* is another book that will make the gatekeepers very unhappy, for it uncovers important details about America's sixteenth president that the Lincoln cult has effectively swept under the rug—until now. The book grew out of my continued interest in the Lincoln legacy after the publication of *The Real Lincoln*. In the years since I wrote that book I have continued to research the issue and discovered entirely new subjects and perspectives on Lincoln, which are presented here for the first time.

The book is divided into three sections: "What You're Not Supposed to Know About Lincoln and His War"; "Economic Issues You're Supposed to Ignore"; and "The Politics of the Lincoln Cult." The first section, Chapters 2 through 10, explores a number of historically important issues that most Americans seem totally unaware of, thanks to the efforts of the gatekeepers.

Chapter 2 runs through "the Lincoln myths"—the most fundamental misconceptions about our sixteenth president.

Chapter 3 reveals that a host of familiar "Lincoln quotes" are, in fact, fake—Lincoln never said them. Academic researchers have exposed the truth that the Lincoln cult wants to obscure. The point is, not only have whole sections of Lincoln's record been expunged from history, but other sections have been fabricated.

Chapters 4 and 5 expose how historians have rewritten antebellum history to portray—falsely—the North as benevolent and benighted, and to demonize the South. In war, the victors get to rewrite the history. Scholars are finally correcting the record. Drawing partly on the work of Brown University historian Joanne Pope Melish, Chapter 4 details how slavery existed in the North for some two hundred years, finally ending in the late 1850s. Thus, nineteenth-century "Yankees" were never quite as morally superior as they made themselves out to be. And as Chapter 5 reveals, Lincoln himself, for his entire adult life, advocated the deportation (his own word) of blacks to Africa, Haiti, Central and South America, and elsewhere. In fact, he held a White House meeting to encourage a group of free black men to "lead by example" and leave the country, moving to Liberia.

There was much more Northern opposition to Lincoln and his war than most Americans know of. Chapter 6 discusses the fiery attacks on Lincoln and his administration by the famous Massachusetts abolitionist Lysander Spooner. Spooner, among the most prominent and active of all the New England abolitionists, believed that the North fought the war to consolidate political power for the benefit of Northern industrialists. He believed—even years after the war—that the issue of slavery was cynically used as a mere political smoke screen.

Generations of Americans have been miseducated about "states' rights," and federalism as well, by being told the false tale that the states' rights doctrine was only an excuse for slavery. The truth, as Chapter 7 shows, is that Thomas Jefferson and

James Madison were among the foremost proponents of states' rights, and for reasons that had nothing to do with slavery. Moreover, the states' rights doctrine was embraced by the citizens of *all* states, north and south, until 1865. Indeed, some northern states invoked the doctrine to "nullify" the federal government's Fugitive Slave Act in the years prior to the war.

Chapter 8 uncovers one of the most important negative consequences of the war: the death of states' rights and, particularly, of the founding fathers' notion of "divided sovereignty." This idea, which is often associated with James Madison, was that the federal government could not be trusted to be the arbiter of what limits would be placed on its own powers. The citizens of the free and independent states, as sovereigns, were to have that role under the original Constitution. This ended in 1865, after which the federal government, through the Supreme Court, would decide what limits would be placed on its own powers. Not surprisingly, it has decided that there are, in essence, no limits at all, just as the founders warned. Throughout the twentieth century all the worst tyrants in the world would attack the idea of states' rights and divided sovereignty and champion the cause of consolidated or centralized government.

Chapter 9 explains how Lincoln drove this transformation in American government by asserting the ahistorical argument that the citizens of the states were never sovereign, and that the Constitution was somehow adopted by "the whole people" of the nation. In reality, "the whole people" had nothing at all to do with the adoption of the Constitution.

Chapter 10 tells the story of how, when confronted with an opinion by the chief justice of the United States, Roger B. Taney—that Lincoln's suspension of the writ of habeas corpus was illegal—the president issued an arrest warrant for the judge. The Lincoln cult has disputed the accuracy of this story in the past, but this chapter presents several new, unimpeachable sources that prove it to be true. Lincoln essentially destroyed the separation of powers during his administration by intimidating federal judges — and not just Taney — in this way.

If there is anything that causes the Lincoln cult to become agitated, if not hysterical, it is the suggestion that Abraham Lincoln, like virtually all other politicians in world history, was acutely interested in the accumulation of money and power. The fact is, he was, as Part II of the book demonstrates. For most of his adult life, before jumping to the Republicans, Lincoln was a member of the Whig Party — the party of the moneyed elite in America. He was a wealthy trial lawyer who married into an affluent, slave-owning Kentucky family, the Todds. As a prominent railroad industry attorney he was a consummate political insider in Northern big business circles.

The Lincoln cult has effectively covered up the truth about Lincoln's and the Republican Party's economic policies. Chapter 11 shows how Lincoln's Republican Party used the powers of the central government to benefit its corporate supporters, usually at the expense of the general public. Lincoln himself was what today would be called a "lobbyist" for the railroad industry, as discussed in Chapter 12. He was also an ardent protectionist who spent his entire political career promoting protectionist tariffs, as shown in Chapter 13, and an "inflationist" who favored letting a federal bank print paper money that was not necessarily redeemable in gold or silver, as demonstrated in Chapter 14. Both the Whig and Republican parties used tariffs and paper money to subsidize corporations engaged in "internal improvements" projects.

Part III — "The Politics of the Lincoln Cult" — describes how the cult uses the Lincoln legacy to promote imperialistic, if not totalitarian, policies in today's world. Advocates of an American empire that would wage "perpetual war for perpetual peace," to borrow a phrase from Gore Vidal, hope to use the Lincoln legend to encourage America's youth to participate in such adventures, as discussed in Chapter 15. Chapter 16 reveals how today's enemies of civil liberties take as their model Lincoln's suspension of civil liberties in the North for the duration of his administration.

Even the Pledge of Allegiance is something that has much less to do with expressing love for one's country than more or less blind obedience to the consolidated, centralized state that was created in the aftermath of the War between the States. Most Americans will be surprised to learn in Chapter 17 that the Pledge was authored in 1892 by an avowed socialist named Francis Bellamy who wanted to use it to indoctrinate schoolchildren into the ideology of big government. The founding fathers would have been appalled by such a thing and would likely have rebelled against it.

The Lincoln cult has even used Lincoln's record of imprisoning some of the congressional opposition, such as Congressman Clement L. Vallandigham of Ohio, who was deported in 1863, as evidence that such a practice might well be acceptable today. This sordid story is told in Chapter 18.

The nineteenth and final chapter begins with a survey of some recent books by prominent authors who have seriously challenged the Official View of American History that is presented by the Lincoln cult. Among these authors are *New York Times* editorial writer Steven R. Weisman, University of Virginia historian Michael F. Holt, liberal writer Michael Lind, historian John Steele Gordon, and former U.S. Navy Secretary and novelist James Webb.

Are the gatekeepers losing their influence at last? We can only hope so.

**PART I**

# What You're Not Supposed to Know About Lincoln and His War

# 2

## The Lincoln Myths—Exposed

In *Lincoln, the South, and Slavery,* historian Robert W. Johann-sen wrote that anyone who embarked on a study of Abraham Lincoln "must first come to terms with the Lincoln myth. The effort to penetrate the crust of legend that surrounds Lincoln . . . is both a formidable and intimidating task."[1]

Indeed it is. One reason for this difficulty is that, as in all wars, the victors write the history. The War between the States is no exception; the victorious federal government has seen to it that generations of "court historians" have rewritten the history of the war, especially with regard to the leading figures in that American tragedy, such as Abraham Lincoln. This occurred partly because the government became more and more influential over education in the postwar era, and government always uses public education to aggrandize itself. But the truth is available for anyone who perseveres enough to look for it. Indeed, the true facts are often found in many of the books and articles written by the court historians themselves, although they are usually buried amidst an avalanche of excuses, rationales, and "spin." Let's take a look at some of the more prominent myths.

**Myth #1: "Lincoln invaded the South to free the slaves."** This is another way of saying that slavery was the sole cause of the war, which has recently become the mantra of the Lincoln gatekeepers. The problem for them, however, is that Lincoln never said this and most certainly did not believe it. Nor did anyone else in his government—or in the Northern states. It is unlikely that *anyone* who voted for Lincoln in 1860 did so because he thought the new president would order an army to march south to free the slaves in a war that might cost hundreds of thousands of lives and billions of dollars.

On March 2, 1861, two days before Lincoln's inauguration as president, the U.S. Senate passed a proposed constitutional amendment that read: "No Amendment shall be made to the Constitution which will authorize or give Congress the power to abolish or interfere, within any State, with the domestic institutions thereof, including that of persons held to labor or service by the laws of the State." The U.S. House of Representatives passed the amendment on February 28, 1861. "Domestic institutions" meant slavery.

Two days later, in his first inaugural address, Lincoln promised several times that he had no intention to interfere with Southern slavery, and that even if he did, it would be unconstitutional to do so. He also pledged his support for this amendment, announcing to the world that "holding such a provision [the legality of slavery] to be implied constitutional law, *I have no objection to its being made express and irrevocable*" (emphasis added).

Thus, on the day of his inauguration, Abraham Lincoln did not defend or support the natural, God-given rights of

> Lincoln wanted the Constitution to make slavery "irrevocable."

Southern slaves to life, liberty, and property. Quite the opposite: He supported the "rights" of Southern slave owners to deprive the slaves of those rights. Lincoln was perfectly willing to see Southern slavery persist long past his own lifetime, for all he knew, as long as the Southern states remained in the Union and continued to pay federal taxes.

Lincoln clearly stated the real cause and purpose of the war on numerous occasions, including in his famous August 22, 1862, letter to newspaper editor Horace Greeley. There he wrote, "My paramount objective in this struggle is to save the Union, and it is not either to save or destroy slavery."[2] His objective was to destroy the secession movement by force of arms, period.

The U.S. Congress concurred, announcing to the world on July 22, 1861, that the purpose of the war was *not* "interference with the rights or established institutions of those states"—that is, slavery—"but to preserve the Union with the rights of the several states unimpaired." Thus, according to both President Lincoln and the Congress, *the conflict over states' rights was the sole cause of the war.* The Confederate states believed the Union was voluntary, that governments derived their just powers from the consent of the governed, and that they consequently had a right to secede. Lincoln disagreed, and was willing to wage total war to "prove" himself right. Most gatekeepers today will say that states' rights were, at best, a "figleaf." Or they will peddle the false notion that it was made up as an excuse after the war by disgruntled former Confederates. Either way, they are distorting true history and contradicting Lincoln himself.

**Myth #2: "Lincoln saved the Union."** In reality, Lincoln did more than any other individual to *destroy* the voluntary union of the founding fathers. All of the founding documents—the Articles of Confederation, the Declaration of Independence, the Treaty with Great Britain, the Constitution—refer to the states as "free and independent." That is, the founders construed them as being free and independent of any other state, including the federal government which they—the states—had created as their agent.

The states delegated certain narrowly defined and enumerated powers to the federal government but preserved sovereignty for themselves. The federal Constitution was created by a voluntary association of states and three of them—New York, Rhode Island, and Virginia—explicitly reserved the right to withdraw from the constitutional compact should the federal government ever abuse their liberties. Since all states have equal rights under the Constitution, and no state is given more rights than any other, the fact that this contingency was accepted by all the other states implies that this right of secession was naturally assumed to be enjoyed by *all* the states. The citizens of the states did not create "a new nation" with the Constitution; they created a compact or a confederacy of states.

This was an uncontroversial view in 1860. Newspapers throughout the North echoed the opinion of the *Bangor Daily Union,* which editorialized on November 13, 1860, that the Union "depends for its continuance on the free consent and will of the sovereign people of each state, and when consent and will is withdrawn on either part, their Union is gone."[3]

Thus, Lincoln "saved" the federal union in the same sense that a man who has been abusing his wife "saves" his marital union by violently forcing his wife back into the home and threatening to shoot her if she leaves again. The union may well be saved, but it is not the same kind of union that existed on their wedding day. That union no longer exists. The American union of the founding fathers ceased to exist in April of 1865.

> The voluntary union of the founding fathers was destroyed in 1865.

**Myth #3: "Lincoln was a champion of the Constitution."** George Orwell himself would blush at this assertion. The only way one could conceivably make this argument is to base the argument exclusively on a few nice things that Lincoln *said* about the Constitution while generally ignoring his *actions*. For example, he launched an invasion without the consent of Congress; illegally suspended the writ of habeas corpus and imprisoned tens of thousands of Northern political opponents; shut down some three hundred opposition newspapers; censored all telegraph communication; imprisoned a large percentage of the duly elected legislature of Maryland as well as the mayor of Baltimore; illegally orchestrated the secession of West Virginia; deported the most outspoken member of the Democratic opposition, Congressman Clement L. Vallandigham of Ohio; systematically disarmed the border states in violation of the Second Amendment; and effectively declared himself dictator. The gatekeepers try to excuse all of this, but their words ring hollow to anyone familiar with the historical facts.

**Myth #4: "Lincoln was devoted to equality."** Lincoln's words and, more important, his *actions,* thoroughly contradict this claim. "I have no purpose to introduce political and social equality between the white and black races," he stated in his August 21, 1858, debate with Stephen Douglas. Incredibly, various Lincoln scholars take a statement like this and somehow conclude that Lincoln "really" meant, "I *do* have purpose to introduce political and racial equality. . . ." Mostly, statements like this are simply ignored and kept from the innocent eyes of American schoolchildren.

> Lincoln's usurpations of power were unconstitutional.

Lincoln opposed the immigration of black people into

Illinois; supported the Illinois Black Codes, which deprived the small number of free blacks who resided in the state of any semblance of citizenship; and was a leader of the Illinois Colonization Society, which persuaded the state legislature to allocate funds to "colonize," or deport, free blacks. As syndicated columnist Joseph Sobran has remarked, Lincoln's position was that blacks could be "equal" all right, but not in the United States. He favored "colonizing" them in Africa, Haiti, Central and South America—anywhere but in the United States. This position was supported by the vast majority of Northerners, and Lincoln, as an astute and even brilliant politician, supported it as well.

**Myth #5: "Lincoln was a great statesman."** Imagine that California seceded from the union and an American president responded with the carpet bombing of Los Angeles, San Diego, and San Francisco that destroyed 90 percent of those cities. Such was the case with General Sherman's bombardment of Atlanta; a naval blockade; a blocking off of virtually all trade; the eviction of thousands of residents from their homes (as occurred in Atlanta in 1864); the destruction of most industries and farms; massive looting of private property by a marauding army; and the killing of one out of four males of military age while maiming for life more than double that number.

> As a man of his time, Lincoln held views that can only be described as the views of a white supremacist.

Would such an American president be considered a "great statesman" or a war criminal? The answer is obvious. A statesman would have recognized the state's right to secede, as enshrined in the Tenth Amendment, among other places, and then worked diligently to persuade the seceded state that a reunion was in its best interest. A great statesman, or even a modest one, would not have impulsively plunged the entire nation into a bloody war.

Lincoln's warmongering belligerence and his invasion of all the Southern states in response to Fort Sumter (where no one was harmed or killed) caused the upper South—Virginia, North Carolina, Tennessee, and Arkansas—to secede after originally voting to remain in the Union. He refused to meet with Confederate commissioners to discuss peace and even declined a meeting with Napoleon III of France, who offered to broker a peace agreement. No genuine statesman would have behaved in such a way.

> A "great statesman" would not have manipulated his own people into the bloodiest war in world history.

After Fort Sumter, Lincoln thanked naval commander Gustavus Fox for assisting him in manipulating the South Carolinians into firing at Fort Sumter. A great statesman does not manipulate his own people into starting one of the bloodiest wars in human history.

**Myth #6: "Lincoln was a great humanitarian."** Great humanitarians do not micromanage the waging of total war, or wage war on civilians, as Lincoln did for the duration of his administration. This included the burning of entire towns populated only by civilians, massive looting and plundering, and even the execution of civilians. A great humanitarian would not express his personal thanks and "the thanks of a nation" to those who committed such atrocities and war crimes, as Lincoln did to General Philip Sheridan. Nor would he have literally laughed at the fate of Southern civilians who had lost everything, as General Sherman said that he did in his [Sherman's] memoirs.

Great humanitarians do not become obsessed with allocating tax dollars to the development of more powerful and more devastating weapons of mass destruction to be aimed at their own citizens, as Lincoln did. Historian Lee Kennett was right when he wrote, in *Marching Through Georgia,* that had the Confederates somehow won, they would have been justified in "stringing up President Lincoln and the entire Union high command" as war criminals, especially for waging war on civilians.[4] This is the kind of conclusion that one often comes to from studying the actual history of the War between the States, as opposed to the fanciful reinterpretations of it provided to us by the gatekeepers and other assorted court historians.

> Humanitarians do not wage war on innocent civilians.

# 3

## Fake Lincoln Quotes

Why is it so difficult to see through, as Robert Johannsen put it, "the crust of legend that surrounds Lincoln"? One reason is that literature is filled with fake Lincoln quotes. These fake statements are used to further advance the deification of the sixteenth president, or to promote a particular political agenda. For example, such a quotation appeared in a 2003 *New York Times* review of a book entitled *Wealth and Democracy: A Political History of the Rich*, by Kevin Phillips. Reviewer Paul Kennedy, a Harvard University historian, repeated a bogus quotation that Phillips used in his book: "The money power preys upon the nation in times of peace, and it conspires against it in times of adversity. It's more despotic than monarchy. It's more insolent than autocracy. It's more selfish than bureaucracy. . . . Corporations have been enthroned, and an era of corruption in high places will follow."

Phillips apparently thought he had found the perfect quotation that attached the "moral authority" of Lincoln to his general theme of "the money power" corrupting society. But as historian Mathew Pinkser wrote on the website History News

Network, the quotation "is nowhere in Lincoln's collected works," and the editor of *Lincoln's Collected Works* called it "a bold, unblushing forgery."

Anyone who knows about the real Lincoln would suspect the quotation to be a forgery. The truth is, Lincoln was a corporate trial lawyer whose clients included every major railroad corporation in the Midwest. At the 1860 Republican National Convention, corporations seeking protectionist trade policies delivered to Lincoln the steel-industry-dominant state of Pennsylvania. He was closely associated with the nation's largest corporations, who were among his staunchest political supporters. It is hardly likely that he would have been on record as expressing such socialistic, antibusiness views as those held by Kevin Phillips, Ralph Nader, and Michael Moore.

And there are dozens, if not hundreds, of quotes like this one that have been used for generations to enhance the "holy" image of the Fake Lincoln. Some of these fraudulent statements are catalogued in an Oxford University Press book entitled *They Never Said It: A Book of Fake Quotes, Misquotes, and Misleading Attributions,* by Professors Paul F. Boller, Jr., and John George.

> Many of your favorite Lincoln quotes are simply fakes.

For decades, scholars and journalists have been quoting Lincoln as saying, "All that loves labor serves the nation. All that harms labor is treason to America. No line can be drawn between these two. If any man tells you he loves America, yet hates labor, he is a liar. If any man tells you he trusts America, yet fears labor, he is a fool. There is no America without labor, and to fleece one is to rob the other."

Labor unions have naturally repeated this quotation endlessly. Unfortunately for them, write Professors Boller and

George, "there is no record of [Lincoln's] ever having uttered these words."[1]

The antiprohibitionist movement has long touted another supposed Lincoln quote: "Prohibition will work great injury to the cause of temperance . . . for it . . . attempts to control a man's appetite by legislation, and makes a crime out of things that are not crimes." "There is no record of this statement being made by Lincoln," write Boller and George.[2] The statement was apparently fabricated by a Georgia antiprohibition leader.

"If I ever get a chance to hit that thing, I'll hit it hard," Lincoln supposedly said about slavery. This, too, is often repeated. In the March 2003 issue of *The American Enterprise* magazine, which was devoted to essays about Lincoln and the War between the States, historian Jay Winik, author of *April 1865: The Month That Saved America,* repeated it. Unfortunately for Winik, Lincoln "never made the above statement," as Boller and George document.[3]

Lincoln never became a Christian, never joined a church, and rarely stepped foot in one, despite his skilled use of religious rhetoric in political speeches. When he ran for president, almost every one of the ministers in Springfield, Illinois, opposed him. Yet he supposedly said, "I have never known a worthwhile man who became too big for his boots or his Bible." Another fake, as Boller and George prove.[4]

The same can be said of the story that, after viewing the graves at Gettysburg, Lincoln became a Christian. He supposedly said, "I then and there consecrated myself to Christ. Yes, I do love Jesus!" Another fake. He never said it. This particular delusion was most likely the result of the successful crusade by the New England clergy after the war to deify Lincoln. They compared him to Jesus and Moses, claiming that just as Jesus died for the world's sins, Lincoln died for the nation's sins. That's why he is sometimes given the blasphemous label of "redeemer president."[5] And just as Moses led his people to the Promised Land but never reached there himself, the same was true of Lincoln. The problem facing the late-nineteenth-century New England clergy, however, was that their "sainted" Lincoln was either an agnostic or an atheist. Thus, he had to be born again— firguratively speaking—as a Christian. As one well-informed clergyman said in mockery, Lincoln became a Christian "six months after his death."[6]

> The old story about Lincoln becoming a Christian in Gettysburg is untrue.

Even though Lincoln was one of the highest-paid trial lawyers in the nation before becoming president and was married to the daughter of a wealthy slave-owning Kentucky family, he is still portrayed as a poor, backwoods "railsplitter" and "a man of the people." Generations of American schoolchildren have been taught that he said, "God must have loved the common people, he made so many of them." There is absolutely no evidence "that Lincoln ever said anything of the kind," conclude Professors Boller and George.[7] They discovered that the origin of this particular fake quotation is a book entitled *Our Presidents* by James Morgan, published in 1928.

"If this nation is to be destroyed," Lincoln is credited with saying, "it will be destroyed from within; if it is not destroyed from within, it will live for all time to come." Another proven fake. Boller and George discovered that this fake quote was a distortion of Lincoln's words by former U.S. Senator Joseph McCarthy in a 1953 speech.[8]

Lincoln was clearly opposed to racial equality of any kind. He stated his opposition to racial equality in many of his public speeches and, more important, demonstrated it through his *actions*. Americans have been misled about his racial beliefs by generations of court historians and gatekeepers. If you've ever read the following quotation attributed to Lincoln you should know that it, too, is a fake: "The restoration of the Rebel States to the Union must rest upon the principle of civil and political equality of both races." He never said it. Nor did he ever say, "Know there is a God and that He hates injustice and slavery," another fake quotation that schoolchildren have been exposed to, say Professors Boller and George.[9]

There are long, words-of-wisdom quotes attributed to Lincoln that make him seem exceptionally wise and sage. These include the admonitions that "You cannot bring about prosperity by discouraging thrift; strengthen the weak by weakening the strong; help strong men by tearing down big men; help the wage earner by pulling down the wage payer; further the brotherhood of man by encouraging class hatred; help the poor by destroying the rich; establish sound security on borrowed money; keep out of trouble by spending more than you earn; build character and courage by taking away man's initiative; and help men permanently by doing for them what they could do for themselves."

These are indeed words of wisdom; every bit of this advice is as sound as a gold dollar. But none of them came from Lincoln. They have all been exposed "as forgeries."[10]

Abraham Lincoln never even said, "You can fool all the people some of the time and some of the people all of the time, but you can not fool all the people all the time." (Besides, his actions and his political rhetoric prove that he did in fact believe it was possible to "fool all the people.") This statement "cannot be found in any of Lincoln's printed addresses," say Boller and

George, yet Lincoln scholars still utilize it because it sounds "Lincolnesque."[11]

Americans are not only unaware of some of the most important facts about Lincoln, as discussed in the last chapter and throughout this book, but much of what they think they know about him is false. They have been very thoroughly miseducated.

# 4

## The Myth of the Morally Superior "Yankee"

I was born and raised in Pennsylvania but do not consider myself to be a Yankee. The word *Yankee* refers not so much to native-born residents of the northern United States, but to an attitude, or mind-set. Dutch immigrants from New York first gave the name to English settlers in Connecticut. In the early to mid-nineteenth century the word gained popularity as a description of a brand of New Englander and, later, midwesterner. The word *Yankee* was attached to those New Englanders who were seen as arrogant, unfriendly, condescending, intolerant, extremely self-righteous, and believing that they were God's chosen people. (Conservative historian Clyde Wilson has remarked that Hillary Clinton, born in Illinois and educated in Massachusetts and Connecticut, is a "museum-quality specimen" of a Yankee.)[1]

Yankees never shied away from using the coercive powers of government to compel others to be remade in their image. Consequently, it is probably not just a coincidence that compulsory government schooling began in New England, as did prohibition. The latest manifestation of the Northern Yankee is "neoconservatism," an ideology that believes the U.S. government should use its military might to remake the entire world in its image, all in the name of "democracy and freedom."

The idea of Yankee moral superiority was carefully crafted from the time of the Pilgrims. By 1861, New England Yankees and their midwestern brethren had concocted the myth of a morally superior free, white, and virtuous New England that had a right to remake other sections of the United States in its own image, creating nothing less than heaven on Earth through the New Englandization of America. A corollary of this notion was the assumption that the slave-owning South was inherently morally inferior.

But the notion of a morally superior New England Yankee society is a myth, as explained in great detail by Brown University professor Joanne Pope Melish in her book *Disowning Slavery: Gradual Emancipation and Race in New England, 1780–1860,* published in 1998 by Cornell University Press. Professor Melish documents how New England opinion makers rewrote their own history (not unlike how the Soviets rewrote theirs) to say that slavery in their part of the country was very brief and relatively benevolent.

Not all Northerners were (or are) "Yankees."

The truth is that slavery existed in New England for more than two hundred years (beginning in 1638) and was as degrading and dehumanizing as slavery elsewhere. In mid-eighteenth-century Rhode Island, slaves accounted for one-third of the population of many communities. Newport, Rhode Island, and Boston, Massachusetts, were the two biggest centers of the transatlantic slave trade. Slave labor was used to build the New England slave ships that transported most of the slaves from Africa.

Virtually all of the New England aristocracy's household and farm labor was done by slaves, Professor Melish writes. "These servants performed the dirty, heavy, dangerous, menial jobs around the household, or they acted in inferior roles as valets and maids to masters and mistresses of the upper class."[2]

Professor Melish also documents the pervasive sexual abuse of female slaves by their New England masters. The renowned New England cleric Cotton Mather advised his fellow Yankees that Christianizing their slaves would transform them into even better slaves. "Your servants will be the Better Servants," the New England religious icon said, "for being made Christian servants."[3] Christianize them, and they will be "afraid of speaking or doing any thing that may justly displeasure you."

> Slavery existed in New England for more than two hundred years and was as degrading and dehumanizing as slavery anywhere.

Slavery became uneconomical in New England with the growth of a manufacturing industry that required a more educated and skilled workforce. And beginning in the late eighteenth century, gradual emancipation laws were introduced. In general, these laws stated that the children of existing slaves would be freed upon reaching a certain age, usually twenty-one to twenty-five. In theory, a one-year-old slave in the year 1784 who had a child at age twenty-five would remain a slave for life, but her child would be freed somewhere around 1834.

Slaves were included in the New England population census during the nineteenth century, and the data reveal that as late as 1848, Rhode Island was passing new laws outlawing slavery. New Hampshire passed a new law outlawing slavery even later—in 1857. Thus, there were still slaves in New Hampshire on the eve of the War between the States. There were slaves in the state of New York until at least 1850, and New Jersey did not end slavery until 1865.[4]

Professor Melish writes of New England slave owners who violated the gradual emancipation laws by keeping their slaves in ignorance of the laws requiring it, or never telling them exactly when they were born so they could be enslaved as long as possible. Many New Englanders did not free their slaves when they reached the age of liberation, but sold them instead to Southern plantation owners. Slavery may have ended, but not all Northern slave owners freed their slaves.

> When New England ever so gradually ended slavery for economic reasons, many New England slave owners sold their slaves to Southern plantation owners.

In *Democracy in America* Tocqueville noted that, ironically, the "problem of race" seemed to be worse in the non-slave-owning states than in slave-owning states. He was aware of the general attitude in New England that all blacks were "aliens" and should be deported or "colonized" back to Africa. Ralph Waldo Emerson proved Tocqueville's point by predicting that as an "inferior" race, blacks would "follow the Dodo into extinction."[5]

Even after gradual emancipation laws were passed New England governments passed legislation that assured "free" blacks would never be granted any semblance of real citizenship. "A complicated system of seizures, fines, whippings, and other punishments for a legion of illegal activities" on the part of free blacks was imposed.[6] Free blacks were denied titles to property, which pauperized them. Vagrancy laws were passed so that New England communities could deport as many free blacks as possible. The free blacks were routinely accused of "disturbing the peace" and subsequently deported out of their communities.

The "morally superior" New England Yankees announced repeatedly that they did not believe black people were capable of citizenship and tried to force them out of their communities. The American Colonization Society, which raised funds to deport blacks to Liberia and other foreign lands, was very active in New England. By 1861 some twelve thousand free blacks from New England had been deported to Liberia, where most of them perished. To New Englanders "abolitionism" did not necessarily mean freedom, it meant "abolishing" the presence of black people from their midst. They were God's chosen people, and no "inferior beings" were acceptable to them. As Ralph Waldo Emerson said, "the abolitionist wishes to abolish slavery, but because he wishes to abolish the black man."[7] That would supposedly "restore New England to an idealized original state as an orderly, homogenous, white society. A free New England would be a white New England."[8] In other words, they apparently hoped to create a superior master race.

In the first half of the nineteenth century, Melish documents that free blacks in New England were horribly abused in inhumane ways. New Englanders were bombarded with graphic literary representations of blacks as preposterous, stupid, or evil beings. There was even a New England version of the Ku Klux Klan terrorist gang long before any such thing appeared in the Southern states. Melish writes of roving gangs that conducted "terroristic raids on urban black communities and the institutions that served them."[9]

Free blacks in New England were urged to leave the country, attacked, rioted against, excluded from juries, and even from cemeteries. Black graves were dug up so that white cemeteries would not be "tainted." "The corpses of people of color seem to have become a target of grave robbers," writes Melish.[10] Black children were excluded from most public schools, even if their parents were taxpayers.

In an early example of the Shermanesque warfare that would

later be used on Southern civilians, entire black communities in New England were assaulted and burned to the ground. "By the early 1820s whites had begun to apply a strategy for their [blacks'] physical removal—assaulting their communities, burning down their homes, and attacking their advocates."[11] There was "a crescendo of mob violence against people of color" in the 1830s, and almost a hundred violent incidents recorded between 1820 and 1840. Morally superior, indeed.

This violence was motivated by the fundamental New England belief that black people were "anomalous and troublesome strangers." Its objective was that "Negroes would slowly diminish in number until finally they would disappear altogether."

By 1853 Frederick Douglass surveyed the situation in New England and asked, "What stone has been left unturned to degrade us? What hand refused to inflame the popular prejudice against us? What whit has not laughed at us in our wretchedness?"[12]

> New Englanders did everything they could to eradicate free blacks from their midst, including burning down entire communities.

Just as Abraham Lincoln never accepted responsibility for the war, essentially blaming it all on God in his second inaugural address, New Englanders never accepted any blame for the sorry plight of the free blacks who lived among them. The reason black people in New England lived a degraded existence, they said, was because of Southern slavery! The idea was repeated enough that it took hold in New England and exists to this day. Melish cites contemporary left-wing "social scientists" (from New England) who claim that northern racism today is not the fault of the northerners themselves; rather, such attitudes are imported from the southern states.

Right-wing economist Thomas Sowell made this same argument in a 2005 book entitled *Black Rednecks and White Liberals,* in which he blames the current problems of northern black communities on seventeenth-century Southern culture. He believes the ancient habits and folkways of the South are still so influential that they control the behavior of entire regions of *the north* today. (Conservatives like Sowell used to champion individual responsibility and excoriate "liberals" who searched for "root causes" of deviant behavior. No longer, at least in Sowell's case.) The perpetual demonization of the South and Southerners is part and parcel of the Lincoln myth. The continued demonization of everything Southern is part of the gatekeepers' strategy to keep the public from ever becoming curious about alternative interpretations of nineteenth-century history.

By 1860 the myth of the morally superior Yankee had migrated to the Midwest along with thousands of transplanted New Englanders. New England attitudes toward blacks were transferred to states such as Illinois, "Land of Lincoln," which in 1848 amended its constitution to prohibit the immigration of black people into the state. Throughout the Midwest, just as in New England, blacks were denied genuine citizenship and discriminated against even more viciously. One of eleven managers of the Illinois Colonization Society, Abraham Lincoln supported allocating state tax dollars for deporting free blacks out of his state.

As early as 1784, reports Professor Melish, an American dictionary quoted a British visitor to America observing that New Englanders were disliked by the inhabitants of all other provinces, "by whom they are called Yankeys. . . ." Little wonder. The North's victory in the War between the States, writes Melish, marked "the stunning success of the cultural imperialism" that was part and parcel of New England nationalism.

At that point, "New England had become the nation and, in the process, the nation had become New England."[13]

> New England's "cultural imperialism" is based on a bundle of lies.

This truth has been swept under the rug by generations of gatekeepers, but it *is* possible to pick up the "rug" and look under it, as Professor Melish demonstrates. Earlier writers have done the same but have been largely ignored. In *The Strange Career of Jim Crow,* first published in 1955, C. Vann Woodward anticipated many of Professor Melish's claims. He noted that the farther west one went, the *worse* things got for blacks. Indiana, Illinois, and Oregon amended their constitutions so that it would be illegal for blacks to immigrate into those states. "Racial discrimination was the rule" in the North, according to Woodward.[14]

Free blacks in the North were basically locked out of the legal system: Only 6 percent of the free blacks in the North lived in states that allowed them to vote; they were generally barred from being jurors; in many states they could not legally testify in court against a white man; and there were "disproportionate numbers of Negroes in Northern prisons. . . ."[15] On the eve of the Civil War, Woodward wrote, the North's position on racial matters was "white supremacy, Negro subordination, and racial segregation." Moreover, "the political party [Republicans] that took control of the federal government at that time was in accord with this position, and *Abraham Lincoln as its foremost spokesman was on record with repeated endorsements*" (emphasis added).[16]

Even the notorious Black Codes that were put into place in the South after the war were not the work of Southerners, but of "the provisional legislatures established by President Johnson in 1865. Some of them were intended to establish systems of peonage or apprenticeship resembling slavery."[17] They were, in other words, the work of the party of Lincoln.

Another author who dared to reveal these truths was historian Leon Litwack, author of the 1961 book *North of Slavery: The Negro in the Free States, 1790–1860.* This book is well known by Lincoln scholars, but it is steadfastly kept from the prying eyes of the general public. "The Mason-Dixon line is a convenient but often misleading geographical division," Litwack wrote.[18] The generally accepted view among most Americans about "southern racial inhumanity" versus "northern benevolence and liberality" in the eighteenth and nineteenth centuries simply "does not accord with the realities. . . ."[19] Moreover, "Abraham Lincoln, in his vigorous support of both white supremacy and denial of equal rights for Negroes, simply gave expression to almost universal American convictions."[20] Most Northerners, Litwack pointed out, favored either voluntary "colonization" or the forced expulsion of all blacks from the United States.

More recently, the New-York Historical Society had an exhibition on the topic of "Slavery in New York" (in late 2005–2006). A book by the same title was published that explains the eye-opening exhibit. As stated in the book's introduction:

> The notorious Black Codes originated in the Northern states and were imposed on the South by the Republican Party's "Reconstruction" governments.

> For nearly three hundred years, slavery was an intimate part of the lives of all New Yorkers, black and white. . . . For portions of the seventeenth and eighteenth centuries, New York City housed the largest urban slave population in mainland North America, with more slaves than any other city on the continent. During those years, slaves composed

more than one quarter of the labor force in the city and perhaps as much as one half of the workers in many of its outlying districts. . . . Slaves could be found in New York into the fifth decade of the nineteenth century.[21]

Also in 2005, Anne Farrow, Joel Lang, and Jenifer Frank, journalists who write for the *Hartford Courant*, published *Complicity: How the North Promoted, Prolonged, and Profited from Slavery.* Several centuries of Northern slavery "has mostly been a shameful and well-kept secret," they write.[22] They point out that it was Massachusetts, not South Carolina, that first legalized slavery. Colonial Boston was "a bustling port for the trade of human flesh." In Rhode Island, "large landholdings used sizable numbers of slaves to provision the . . . plantations in the Caribbean with foodstuffs."[23]

Rhode Island was long the leader in the transatlantic slave trade. Although the transatlantic slave trade was made illegal in the United States in 1808, in 1860 *and beyond* Manhattan shipyards continued to build slave ships that were used to transport slaves from Africa to the Caribbean and elsewhere.[24] It was Harvard University researchers who established the discredited field of "race science" in the nineteenth century that was used to justify slavery and the subordination of black people.

Several decades after the end of the War between the States, Connecticut businessmen operated an "international center for ivory production" in their state, "through the enslavement . . . of as many as 2 million people—in Africa."[25]

Not surprisingly, "Northerners have pushed much of their early history into the deepest shadows of repression."[26] The New England version of mid-nineteenth-century American history, with its heroic, freedom-loving North and evil South, is "a convenient and whitewashed shorthand, at best."[27] Yet it is the history that has been taught to American schoolchildren for generations, indoctrinating the America public in the myth of the morally superior Yankee.

# 5

## Lincoln's Liberian Connection

*Ebony* magazine editor Lerone Bennett, Jr., harshly criticized Lincoln in his book *Forced into Glory: Abraham Lincoln's White Dream,* because of Lincoln's lifelong advocacy of "colonization." He recommended deporting black people to some other country—Africa, Haiti, Central America—anywhere outside the United States.[1]

One of Lincoln's first choices was the West African country of Liberia, created in 1816 by the American Colonization Society, which had purchased land for the purpose of "colonizing" black Americans there. One of the founders, and eventual presidents, of the society was Henry Clay, Lincoln's professed political role model whom he idolized as "the father of Whig principles." Lincoln followed in his idol's footsteps, being appointed as one of eleven managers of the Illinois Colonization Society.[2]

As president, Lincoln tried repeatedly to get a colonization program going, which he eventually did. In 1862 he invited a group of free black men into the White House to request that they lead by example and leave the country.[3] The men were greeted by the federal commissioner of emigration, J. Mitchell. Lincoln informed the men that, at his request, a sum of money had been appropriated by Congress "for the purpose of aiding the colonization in some country of the people, or portion of them, of African descent." Thus, early in his administration Lincoln commenced a plan to eventually ship all black people out of the country. This is what Lerone Bennett, Jr., called Lincoln's "white dream."

"You and we are different races," Lincoln astutely observed. "We have between us a broader difference than exists between almost any other two races. . . . This physical difference is a great disadvantage to us both" and "affords a reason at least why we should be separated. . . . It is better for us both, therefore, to be separate."[4]

Lincoln was a manager of the Illinois Colonization Society, which sought to deport all of the state's free black people.

The president then made his sales pitch for Liberia: "The colony of Liberia has been in existence a long time. In a certain sense it is a success. The old president of Liberia, Roberts, has just been with me—the first time I ever saw him. He says they have within the bounds of that colony between 300,000 and 400,000 people. . . . They are not all American [black] colonists, or their descendants. Something less than 12,000 have been sent hither from this country. Many of the original settlers have died, yet like people elsewhere, their offspring outnumber those deceased."[5]

This was not an offer one would jump at. Lincoln was telling the men that if they went to Liberia, most of them would probably die within a few years. But, if they procreated in the meantime, several decades hence their descendants would likely outnumber them. Little wonder Frederick Douglas had nothing but scorn for Lincoln's colonization schemes, and abolitionist William Lloyd Garrison denounced him as not having "a drop of anti-slavery blood in his veins."[6] The leader of the delegation of free black men, Mr. E. M. Thomas, promised a response to Lincoln's proposal but there is no record of one being received.

Lead by example, Lincoln told a contingent of free black men in the White House, and migrate to Liberia.

This incident was not a onetime flight of fancy for Lincoln. In his July 6, 1852, eulogy to Henry Clay, delivered in Springfield, Illinois, Lincoln approvingly quoted Clay's statement that "there is a moral fitness in the idea of returning to Africa her children," which would supposedly be "a signal blessing to that most unfortunate region." He first proposed deporting American blacks to Liberia in an 1854 speech in Peoria, Illinois. On June 26, 1857, as an aside while commenting on the *Dred Scott* decision, Lincoln offered another reason why he favored colonization: "There is a natural disgust in the minds of nearly all white people, to the idea of an indiscriminate amalgamation of the white and black races. . . ."[7] He voiced such opinions throughout his entire adult life. Such views were consistent with the views of the vast majority of white people in the North.

During his administration Lincoln allocated funds to found a colony of American blacks in Haiti, but the crooked businessman Bernard Koch, who was chosen to be the "governor" of the colony, embezzled most of the federally appropriated funds. In 1864 Lincoln finally concluded that the Haitian colonization experiment had failed and instructed the War Department to offer to return the Haitian colonists to the United States.

Lincoln even toyed with the idea of turning American blacks into Panamanian coal miners. Funds were allocated to purchase land for colonization in Panama once large coal deposits were discovered there. The administration's plans to subsidize a transcontinental railroad would require a great deal of coal to fuel the trains, and it would take a lot of backbreaking labor to mine sufficient quantities of the mineral. In the same White House meeting with the free black men where the topic of Liberia was discussed Lincoln told the men that if Liberia was not to their liking, "Room in South America for colonization, can be obtained cheaply, and in abundance."

Panama was a malaria trap when the Panama Canal was dug in the early twentieth century; "colonization" there in the 1860s would have meant the certain demise of the settlers. The delegation of free black men politely turned down Lincoln's offer but, according to historian Webb Garrison, the president continued to plot and plan some kind of colonization program till the end of his presidency.

# 6

An Abolitionist Who Despised Lincoln

The myth of Northern "national unity" is one of the biggest myths surrounding Lincoln and the history of the War between the States. The *truth:* There was a great deal of dissent and political opposition in the North. The Lincoln administration used a variety of tactics to squash dissent: shutting down three hundred opposition newspapers, suspending habeas corpus, imprisoning tens of thousands of political dissenters, deporting outspoken Democratic congressman Clement Vallandigham of Ohio, censoring telegraphs, intimidating judges, conscripting soldiers, recruiting thousands of foreign immigrants to fight in the war, and rigging Northern elections, to name but a few. Lincoln's reliance on these underhanded devices proves there was indeed a great deal of opposition to his administration in the North, which was anything but "unified" in the war effort. Despite all these dictatorial efforts, he still only won 55 percent of the popular vote in the North in 1864.

A dramatic critique of the Lincoln administration came from famed Massachusetts abolitionist, philosopher, and legal scholar Lysander Spooner (1808–1887). Spooner and his family had been abolitionists for decades prior to the war. In 1845 he authored the book *The Unconstitutionality of Slavery*, which made him an instant hero to the abolition movement. The book made a seemingly ironclad case that slavery was unconstitutional, advocated jury nullification of the Fugitive Slave Act (which Lincoln strongly supported), and called for abolitionists to aid and finance slave insurrections in the South. Spooner went so far as to hatch a plot to kidnap Virginia governor Henry Wise and hold him hostage in exchange for John Brown.

Today, libertarians consider Spooner to be one of their heroes and icons. In the introduction to *The Lysander Spooner Reader,* historian and philsopher George H. Smith describes Spooner as "one of the greatest libertarian theorists of the nineteenth (or any other) century."[1] Spooner's "contempt for government was rivaled only by his contempt for fellow libertarians who compromised their principles."[2] Spooner was not a mere theorist of liberty; he founded a private mail delivery service that underpriced the U.S. Postal Service, which he believed was an unconscionable government monopoly that exploited the public.

Lysander Spooner was a hero of the New England abolitionist movement who despised Lincoln and his entire administration.

Lysander Spooner was a fiery and influential opponent of the Republican Party regime in general, and of Abraham Lincoln in particular. Spooner's *Collected Papers* include a January 22, 1860, letter to William Seward of New York, who would become Lincoln's secretary of state and the administrator of a secret police force that rounded up and imprisoned thousands of political dissenters.[3] Like many other Republicans, Seward had spent the previous decade making self-aggrandizing speeches for supposedly being a great defender of human liberty.

Based on Seward's *actions,* as opposed to his political rhetoric, Spooner believed that Seward was a fake and a hypocrite. His letter to Seward leads off with a most incendiary sentence, speaking of "evidence of your unfaithfulness to freedom" and a pledge, by Spooner, to "embarrass the plans of the Chases, and Sumners, and Wilsons, and Hales, and the other Jesuitical leaders of the Republican Party, who profess that they can aid liberty, without injuring slavery."[4] (Note: "Jesuitical" means "crafty and equivocating.")[5]

A good example of why Spooner believed the entire Republican Party cabal was comprised of hypocrites and scoundrels is because they used antislavery language while at the same time working to cement Southern slavery into place permanently through a constitutional amendment. The so-called Lincoln scholars know that not only did Lincoln voice support for the proposed 1861 amendment to the Constitution that would have forbidden the federal government from ever interfering with Southern slavery in his first inaugural address, but that *the amendment was his idea.* Doris Kearns Goodwin, for one, discusses the whole sordid affair in her Lincoln biography, *Team of Rivals.*[6]

As soon as he was elected, but before his inauguration, Lincoln "instructed Seward to introduce [the amendment] in the Senate Committee of Thirteen without indicating they issued from Springfield."[7] Lincoln instructed Seward to begin the procedure to enact a constitutional amendment that would say, "the Constitution should never be altered so as to authorize Congress to abolish or interfere with slavery in the states."[8] In addition, Lincoln instructed Seward to get through Congress a law that would make the various "personal liberty laws" that existed in some Northern states illegal. (Such state laws nullified the federal Fugitive Slave Act, which required Northerners to apprehend runaway slaves.)

Goodwin writes that when Seward announced these actions to a Boston audience he was met with "thunderous applause." Lincoln then personally congratulated him for a job well done.

So despite all their talk of "liberty," and all their "anti-slavery" rhetoric, these kinds of actions proved to Spooner that these men were diabolical liars, connivers, and political manipulators of the worst kind. He excoriated them for believing that they could "ride into power on the two horses of Liberty and Slavery." In his letter to Seward he called the future secretary of state, and the rest of the prominent Republicans, "double-faced demagogues."

> The famous Massachusetts abolitionist condemned the Lincoln regime as full of "fakes and hypocrites."

*The Unconstitutionality of Slavery,* published some fifteen years earlier, had never been refuted in print or in public. Spooner reminded Seward of this, going so far as to point out that Senator Brown of Mississippi had publicly admitted Spooner's arguments to be irrefutable, whereas he (Seward), a supposed champion of "liberty," had not. "Thus an open advocate of slavery from Mississippi virtually makes more concessions to the anti-slavery character of the constitution, than a professed advocate of liberty from New York. . . ."

Spooner closed his letter to Seward—one in a series exchanged between the two—by saying that he intended to make their full correspondence public, contrary to Seward's wishes that it be kept secret and private. This action would have supported Spooner's intention to "serve any purpose towards defeating yourself and the Republicans," upon which time "I shall be gratified."[9]

Two years—and many thousands of war-related deaths—later,

Spooner focused his ire on another Republican Party luminary, Senator Charles Sumner of Massachusetts, who was known to have admitted in public that Spooner's argument on the unconstitutionality of slavery was irrefutable. "Why, then, in Heaven's name, do you not take that position?" he boomed in a letter to the Massachusetts senator. As with Lincoln, Seward, and others, Sumner only "opposed" slavery in the abstract, not in reality. Consequently, wrote Spooner, "while for a dozen years, you have been making the most bombastic pretensions of zeal for freedom, you have really been, all that time, a deliberately perjured traitor to the constitution, to liberty, and to truth." He then accused Sumner of "treason" to the Constitution.[10]

> Spooner never believed the North fought for "liberty and justice" but for "control of [Southern] markets."

Spooner strongly believed that, had the case been publicly made by some of the nation's leading politicians that slavery was unconstitutional, then world opinion would have pressured honorable Southern leaders like Jefferson Davis and Robert E. Lee (who denounced slavery as a "moral and political evil" and emancipated the slaves his wife inherited) to work toward doing what the British, Spanish, Dutch, French, Danes, and others had done during the nineteenth century: end slavery peacefully. In his own words, from the letter to Sumner:

> Had all those men at the North, who believed these ideas [i.e., the unconstitutionality of slavery] to be true, promulgated them as was their plain and obvious duty to do, it is reasonable to suppose that we should long since have had freedom, without shedding one drop of blood . . . the South

could, consistently with honor, and probably would, long before this time, and without a conflict, have surrendered their slavery to the demand of the constitution . . . and to the moral sentiment of the world . . . you, and others like you have done more, according to your abilities, to prevent the peaceful abolition of slavery, than any other men in the nation.[11]

Spooner was not finished. He continued on, criticizing that "in your pretended zeal for liberty, you have been urging the nation to the most frightful destruction of human life," and "through a series of years, betrayed the very citadel of liberty, which you were under oath to defend." There has been "no other treason at all comparable with this."[12]

Now *that* is what is meant by "speaking truth to power." As George H. Smith wrote in the introduction to *The Lysander Spooner Reader,* "Spooner stood nearly alone among radical abolitionists in his defense of the right of the South to secede from the Union."[13] To Spooner, the right of secession was "a right that was embodied in the American Revolution," which was, first and foremost, a war of separation or secession from the British Empire.

In his 1870 essay "No Treason," Spooner revealed that he never changed his opinion of Seward, Sumner, Lincoln, and the entire Republican Party regime. He wrote that the war "erupted for a purely pecuniary consideration," and not for any moral reason. He labeled the economic lifeblood of the Republican Party, Northern bankers, manufacturers, and railroad corporations, "lenders of blood money" who had "for a long series of years previous to the war, been the willing accomplices of the slaveholders in perverting the government from the purpose of

liberty and justice. . . ."[14] It was such interests, after all, that
benefited so handsomely from the transatlantic slave trade and
the cheap cotton that it produced.

To Spooner the Northern financiers of the war who had
lent millions to the Lincoln government did not do so for "any
love of liberty or justice," but for "the control of [Southern]
markets" through tariff "extortion." Mocking the argument of
the "lenders of blood money" as they addressed the South
he wrote: "If you [the South] will not pay us our price [a high
tariff] . . . we will secure the same price (and keep control of your
markets) by helping your slaves against you, and using them as
our tools for maintaining dominion over you; for the control of
your markets. . . ."[15]

In return for financing a large part of Lincoln's war machine,
Spooner noted, "these holders of the debt are to be paid still
further—and perhaps doubly, triply, or quadruply paid—by such
tariffs on imports as will enable our home manufactures to real-
ize enormous prices for their commodities; also by such monopo-
lies in banking as will enable them to keep control of, and thus
enslave and plunder, the industry and trade of the great body of
Northern people themselves."[16] The war had led to "the industrial and commercial slavery" of all Americans, North and
South. Spooner was obviously referring to the fact that, during
the war, the average tariff rate on imported goods was raised to
nearly 50 percent (from a pre-
war low of 15 percent), and remained in that range for the
next five decades.

Spooner called General Grant
"the chief murderer of the war."

Referring to President Ulysses S. Grant, Spooner noted that
the Northern business interests who controlled the Republican
Party had "put their sword into the hands of the chief murderer
of the war," who at the time was hypocritically declaring, "Let

us have peace."[17] General Grant was known for his willingness to send tens of thousands of Northern men, in wave after wave of attack, into the teeth of Robert E. Lee's well-entrenched Army of Northern Virginia, which was extremely proficient at killing them by the thousands. The war became known as a "war of attrition," meaning Grant knew he could conscript an army several times larger than the Confederate army, so his own soldiers' lives were relatively "cheap"—*to him*. He could afford to send tens of thousands to their death as a strategy for victory; the much less heavily populated South could not.

Spooner interpreted the crushing of the Southern secessionists, some three hundred thousand of whom (3 percent of the Southern population) were killed at the hands of "murderers" like Grant, as suggesting that Southerners should "Submit quietly to all the robbery and slavery we have arranged for you, and you can have your peace."[18]

The Republican Party rhetoric of "saving the union" and "abolishing slavery" was all a sham. "The pretense that the 'abolition of slavery' was either a motive or justification for the war, is a fraud of the same character with that of 'maintaining national honor,'" Spooner wrote. The Republicans did not end slavery "as an act of justice to the black man himself, but only as a 'war measure,'" he wrote, using the exact words ("war measure") that Lincoln himself used in the Emancipation Proclamation. They did this, said Spooner, because "they wanted his [the black man's] assistance . . . in carrying on the war they had undertaken for maintaining and intensifying that political, commercial, and industrial slavery."[19]

Spooner understood that if the Republicans wanted to abolish slavery and not anything else, then a road map for doing so was readily available to them: They could follow the lead of the rest of the civilized world and end slavery peacefully through some plan for compensated emancipation. Lincoln did talk about such a plan, but failed to use his legendary political skills to see it through to success.

The Massachusetts abolitionist also ridiculed Lincoln's quite absurd statement in the Gettysburg Address that he had been waging war for the principle of "a government of consent." In reality, the "consent" Lincoln advocated was: "Everybody must consent, or be shot." This idea "was the dominant one on which the war was carried on."[20] Thus, "all of these cries of having abolished slavery, of having saved the country, of having preserved the union, of establishing a government of consent and maintaining the national honor, are all gross, shameless, transparent cheats."[21]

> The great abolitionist claimed that the abolition of slavery was never the true reason for the war.

Walt Whitman would echo Spooner's opinions, but in a somewhat more approving way. In *The Lysander Spooner Reader* George H. Smith quotes Whitman as saying, "The war taught America that a nation cannot be trifled with."[22] That is, the logo of the U.S. government became: "Consent to our mandates or be shot." New England ministers went even further, deifying both Lincoln and the American state. Smith quotes Unitarian minister Henry Bellows as announcing after the war, "The state is indeed divine, as being the great incarnation of a nation's rights, privileges, honor, and life."

This type of thinking was a direct repudiation of the "natural rights" philosophy of the founding fathers, which held that human rights to life, liberty, and property are inalienable and *God-given,* and are not handed down by *any* state. In the name of religion, ministers like Bellows literally claimed that politicians who ran the federal government should justifiably take the place of God as the source of all human rights.

This literal deification of the state went a long way toward helping the astonishing growth of the power of government that would occur in the postwar years, something that would not have been at all surprising to Lysander Spooner.

# 7

## The Truth About States' Rights

In his first inaugural address Abraham Lincoln made the absurd assertion that the Union preceded the states, and, therefore, state sovereignty did not exist. This falsehood has been endlessly repeated by various gatekeepers and other advocates of militaristic nationalism and executive power for generations. The truth is, to the founding generation, what has variously been called state sovereignty, states' rights, or federalism, was perhaps the most important guarantor of their freedoms as American citizens.

It is well known that Southerners from Jefferson to Calhoun to Jefferson Davis championed states' rights in defense of liberty, but less well known is that the states' rights tradition was a powerful force in *Northern* politics as well until 1865. As Dean Sprague wrote in *Freedom Under Lincoln,* "States' rights, which prior to 1860 had been as important a part of northern beliefs as southern, were overturned" by Lincoln's war.[1]

The founding fathers understood that if they were to have a government of consent, the federal government would sometimes have to defer to state sovereignty when challenged. One example is how New Englanders responded to President Thomas Jefferson's trade embargo, which was extremely harmful to the New England shipping industry.

President Jefferson responded the only way he knew how when the conflict between Britain and France led to the confiscation of several American ships by the British. On December 22, 1807, he announced an embargo on all shipping. The New England economy depended heavily on ocean shipping and was crippled by the embargo. The New England states formally "nullified" the embargo law, citing Jefferson's famous Kentucky Resolve of 1798 which enunciated the principle of nullification, or nonenforcement, of a federal law by the citizens of a state.[2] To Jefferson—and the New Englanders of his time—the citizens of the states had every bit as much right as the president, Congress, or the Supreme Court to make judgments on the constitutionality of federal laws and decide for themselves whether or not such laws should be obeyed.

On February 5, 1809, both houses of the Massachusetts legislature nullified the embargo act by denouncing it as "unjust, oppressive, and unconstitutional. While this state maintains its sovereignty and independence, all the citizens can find protection against outrage and injustice in the strong arm of state government."[3] The embargo, said the Massachusetts legislature, "was not legally binding on the citizens of the state."[4]

From the beginning of the Republic, states' rights was an *American* political doctrine, used by Northern and Southern states alike.

Connecticut also denounced the federal embargo law as being "incompatible with the Constitution of the United States, and encroaching upon the immunities of the State."[5] Its legislature directed all state government officials to deny "any official aid or cooperation in the execution of the act aforesaid."

Rhode Island's legislature announced that it was its duty to "interpose for the purpose of protecting [its citizens] from the ruinous inflictions of usurped and unconstitutional power." All of New England, plus the state of Delaware, formally nullified the federal embargo by denouncing it as an unconstitutional usurpation of power, in the spirit of Jefferson's own states' rights dictum, the Kentucky Resolve of 1798. Nullification was an essential part of the American states' rights tradition, and it was utilized by Northern states as much as, if not more than, Southern states prior to 1861.

When the War of 1812 broke out, New England Federalists saw it as primarily a dispute between Jefferson's opposing Democratic-Republican Party and England that did not involve their region of the country (which was heavily involved in trade and commerce with England). Consequently, the region refused to send militia troops when requested by President James Madison. The Connecticut state assembly issued the following statement, a classic example of the states' rights philosophy that John C. Calhoun would later use in his defense of the free-trade South against the protectionist North.

> But it must not be forgotten that the state of Connecticut is a FREE SOVEREIGN and INDEPENDENT State; that the United States are a confederated and not a consolidated Republic. The Governor of this State is under a high and solemn obligation, "to maintain the lawful rights and privileges thereof, as a sovereign, free and independent State," as he is "to support the Constitution of the United States," and the obligation to support the latter imposes an addi-

tional obligation to support the former. The building cannot stand, if the pillars upon which it rests, are impaired or destroyed.[6]

This statement proves the absurdity of Lincoln's claim in his first inaugural address that the states were not sovereign. They certainly were. This was understood by the founding fathers and by statesmen for decades thereafter. Neither President Thomas Jefferson nor his successor, President Madison, believed that they had any authority to use military force to compel a state to abide by their political dictates. In fact, it's impossible to believe that the thought even would have entered their minds.

The embargo, the War of 1812, and the 1803 Louisiana Purchase—three events viewed as politically and economically harmful to their region—so aggravated New Englanders that they plotted to secede for most of the first decade of the nineteenth century (New Englanders opposed the "hordes of foreigners" becoming American citizens that would be the result of the Louisiana Purchase). As Governor Griswold of Connecticut announced, "The balance of power under the present government is decidedly in favor of the Southern states. . . . The extent and increasing population of those states must forever secure to them the preponderance which they now possess. . . . [New Englanders] are paying the principle part of the expenses of government" without receiving commensurate benefits.[7]

The New England secession movement was led by Senator Timothy Pickering of Massachusetts. Pickering had served as General George Washington's adjutant general, and later as President Washington's secretary of state and secretary of war, holding the former position under President John Adams as well. Announcing that secession was "the" principle of the

American Revolution, Pickering said, "I will rather anticipate a new confederacy, exempt from the corrupt and corrupting influence of the aristocratic Democrats of the South."[8]

In 1814 the New England secessionists held a convention in Hartford, Connecticut, where they decided against secession. They did not question the *right* of secession, or the fact that the states were sovereign, only the practical economic and political wisdom of such a move.

Northern states were also instrumental in assisting President Andrew Jackson in his defeat of the Bank of the United States (BUS). The bank, which would later be championed by Lincoln for his entire political career, was notoriously corrupt and politicized. Consequently, a number of states attempted to tax it out of existence. The Ohio legislature enacted a $50,000 per year tax on each of the two branches of the BUS that had opened in that state. The bank refused to pay, and the chief justice of the United States, Judge John Marshall, supported its decision. But Ohio

> New England was the first region of the country to seriously threaten secession, going so far as to hold a secession convention in Hartford in 1814.

didn't consider Marshall's decision anything more than his opinion, and certainly not more authoritative than that of the state's own legislature. Explicitly citing the Kentucky Resolve, along with James Madison's almost identical Virginia Resolve of 1798,[9] the Ohio legislature publicly declared that "the States have an equal right to interpret [the] Constitution for themselves."[10] Ohio withdrew "the protection and aid of the laws of the state" from the bank, and Kentucky, Tennessee, Connecticut, South Carolina, New York, and New Hampshire followed suit.

As early as 1816, Indiana and Illinois amended their state constitutions to prohibit the BUS from establishing branches within their jurisdictions. When Maryland did the same, the federal government brought suit in that state, with the case of *McCulloch v. Maryland.* Knowing that such taxes could destroy the federal government's bank, Chief Justice John Marshall wrote an opinion in the bank's favor, famously commenting that "the power to tax is the power to destroy." Americans who are familiar with this slogan tend to believe that it refers to the ability of government to "destroy" private-sector economic activity. That is true enough, but what Marshall was concerned with was the power of *states' rights* to destroy the Federalists' quest for a monetary monopoly operated out of the nation's capital. It was the central bank that was being threatened with destruction, which is exactly what the citizens of these sovereign states wanted.

At the time, the Supreme Court's pronouncements were not considered the last word on issues of constitutionality, and other states continued to harass the BUS with punitive taxes. In light of Marshall's opinion, the bank refused to pay the $50,000 tax to the state of Ohio, so the state auditor ordered a deputy, John L. Harper, to collect the tax. As James J. Kilpatrick describes the confrontation: "On the morning of September 17, Harper made one last request for voluntary payment. When this was denied, he leaped over the counter, strode into the bank vaults, and helped himself to $100,000 in paper and specie. He then turned this over to a deputy . . . stuffing this considerable hoard into a small trunk, with which the party thoughtfully had come equipped."[11]

The BUS sued Ohio, citing Marshall's opinion. But Ohio considered the bank's heavy-handed imposition into the state as a threat to the liberties of all Americans, not just Ohioans. Consequently, the state's legislature issued a statement saying, "To acquiesce in such an encroachment upon the privileges and authority of the States, without an effort to defend them, would be an act of treachery to the State itself, *and to all the States that compose the American Union*" (emphasis added). The legislature was aware of Marshall's theory that the Supreme Court should have the last word on constitutionality, but declared: "to this doctrine" they "can never give their assent" quoting Jefferson's Kentucky Resolve.[12] The legislature felt no obligation to obey Marshall's ruling.

Ohio then promised to return the $100,000 if the BUS left the state. If not, it proposed a law that would prevent the jailing of any citizen who defied the bank, denouncing the federal courts for "violation of the Constitution." Kentucky, Connecticut, New York, and New Hampshire issued almost identical declarations soon thereafter.

In light of these relentless attacks on the bank, spurred on by the deeply held belief in states' rights, President Andrew Jackson gained the upper hand in his political battle to defund the BUS. Public opinion turned against the bank, and Jackson had his way. The Bank of the United States was not rechartered.

Northern states also relied on the states' rights doctrine of nullification to attempt to nullify the Fugitive Slave Act, which compelled Northern states to capture runaway slaves and return them to their owners. It was natural for them to think of states' rights as a tool to be used for the liberation of runaway slaves.

Nullification and secession were the two most essential elements of the states' rights doctrine prior to 1861. The New England Federalists plotted to secede in response to Jefferson's election, an action they viewed as perfectly consistent with the philosophy and ideals of the American Revolution. Nullification was widely used as a political tool in the North as well. Indeed, on the eve of the war, most Northern newspapers voiced the opinion that the Southern states were perfectly within their

rights to peacefully secede. There was even a vigorous secession movement in the "middle states"—New York, New Jersey,
Pennsylvania, Delaware, and Maryland—in the 1850s.[13] One
thing the residents of the so-called middle states had in common with the South was that many of them wanted no part of a
government that included the domineering, puritanical New
England "Yankees."

## SECTION ONE OF THE
## KENTUCKY RESOLVE OF 1798
*(Authored by Thomas Jefferson)*

November 10, 1798

Resolved, that the several States composing the United States of America, are not united on the principles of unlimited submission to their General Government; but that by compact under the style and title of a Constitution for the United States and of amendments thereto, they constituted a General Government for special purposes, delegated to that Government certain definite powers, reserving each State to itself, the residuary mass of right to their own self Government; and that whensoever the General Government assumes undelegated powers, its acts are unauthoritative, void, and of no force: That to this compact each State acceded as a State, and is an integral party, its co-States forming as to itself, the other party: That the Government created by this compact was not made the exclusive or final *judge* of the extent of the powers delegated to itself; since that would have made its discretion, and not the Constitution, the measure of its powers; but that as in all other cases of compact among parties having no common Judge, each party has an equal right to judge for itself, as well of infractions as of the mode and measure of redress.

# 8

## Constitutional Futility

M any conservatives and libertarians are fond of describing themselves as "strict constructionists," meaning they believe the government should strictly enforce the U.S. Constitution as it reads. They believe that, for far too long, the federal government has been either ignoring the constitutional limitations on its powers, or simply making things up as it goes to rationalize the unconstitutional use of governmental power. Consequently, they tend to speak with great reverence for the Constitution, and the founders, and urge other Americans to do the same. The libertarian Cato Institute in Washington, D.C., even mass distributes pocket-sized replicas of the U.S. Constitution, apparently in the hope that once the public reads the document it will somehow insist that it be enforced.

Though Cato's deed is admirable, nothing could be more naive—or futile. Despite all efforts, the federal government has increased its control over the American educational system, decade by decade, and it is no coincidence that fewer and fewer American students have been educated in the virtues of limited constitutional government. It is simply not in the federal government's self-interest to teach the public that it is advantageous to place limits on the government's powers.

It must be recognized that there is a powerful constituency for ignoring the constitutional limits on governmental powers, and there is no well-organized pressure group of any consequence in favor of it. All special-interest groups seeking a share of federal largesse work diligently, day in and day out, to urge the government to abandon or ignore constitutional limits and award them subsidies. In contrast, the general public is widely dispersed and rarely ever well organized politically. The public would benefit most from constitutional government, but costs overwhelm the effort to coalesce the masses into an effective political pressure group.

Consider the minor example of farm subsidies. One form of such subsidies is price supports on sugar, which are laws that prop up the price of sugar to three to four times the world price. Sugar, and everything made with it, is more expensive to American consumers for no other reason than sugar farmers are fond of plundering their fellow citizens, and are very well organized politically.

For such plunder to end, the individual American consumer would have to spend time, effort, and money to convince a majority of Congress to repeal the sugar price support law. Needless to say, few average citizens would take on this monumental task for the admittedly modest benefit. There are literally thousands of similar programs, none of which are permitted by the Constitution, that are the result of a strong political group legally plundering a weak one, and the American public bears the costs. This is political reality; it is mere fantasy to believe that the general public—in a nation of almost three hundred million people—will someday rise up and demand a return to strict constructionism.

Modern-day strict constructionists are unaware of how the founding fathers intended for the Constitution to be enforced: by the citizens of the free and independent states, not by the federal judiciary or by another organ of the federal government. The Constitution sought not only to limit the federal government by restricting its reach to a narrow list of "enumerated powers" (Article I, Section 8), along with the system of checks and balances, but also with the much more important doctrine of *divided sovereignty.* That is, the citizens of the states were to have an equal voice in constitutional matters. As Johns Hopkins University political theorist Gottfried Dietze wrote in *America's Political Dilemma*: "Federalism, instituted to enable the federal government to check oppressions by the government of the states, *and vice versa,* appears to be a supreme principle of the Constitution" (emphasis added).[1]

In other words, the central government was given certain abilities to police attempted infringements upon the liberties of the people by the state governments; but at the same time, the Tenth Amendment reserved to the states, and their citizens, the right to police or veto unconstitutional or despotic proclivities of the central government. If the American people were to be sovereign over their government, and if the Constitution was to be a meaningful document, this could only be accomplished by the actions of citizens as members of political communities organized at the state and local levels. This is what was meant by "divided sovereignty."

But the founding fathers' system of divided sovereignty, championed by James Madison, was destroyed in 1865. As Professor Dietze further observed: "[B]efore the Civil War . . . the nature of American federalism was still a subject of debate. The outcome of the Civil War ended that debate. The Nationalists emerged as victors. National power increased as the twentieth century approached [along with] the disappearance of states' rights."[2] That period was subsequently characterized by "an increasing interference with economic freedom" and "constitutes a constitutional revolution that can well be termed a reversal of the Revolution of 1787."

With the system of divided sovereignty destroyed, the federal government made itself the sole arbiter of constitutionality, through the U.S. Supreme Court. Not surprisingly, and as the Jeffersonians warned, the federal government has used this role to decide that there are, in fact, no real limits to its powers. Consequently, Americans are no longer sovereign over their government.

> The principle of federalism was essentially a dead letter after 1865.

Indeed, former champions of extraconstitutional governmental powers, such as former President Woodrow Wilson, have long *celebrated* this fact. Before becoming president Wilson was a political science professor at Princeton University and wrote a book entitled *Constitutional Government in the United States*. In it he approvingly proclaimed that "The War between the States established . . . this principle, that the federal government is, through its courts, the final judge of its own powers."[3] This fox-guarding-the-henhouse theory of the Constitution has been a disaster for America, for reasons the founding fathers — especially Jefferson — understood all too well. Indeed, the Jeffersonians in American politics warned against such an outcome for several generations.

## THE LONG-FORGOTTEN JEFFERSONIAN TRADITION

The principle of dual sovereignty was perhaps best expressed, historically, in the applications of the Kentucky and Virginia

Resolves. It is important that in the Kentucky Resolve Jefferson referred to the "United States" in the plural, which is how it is referred to in *all* of the founding documents, including the Declaration of Independence, Treaty with Great Britain, Articles of Confederation, and the Constitution. The obvious reason for this was the clear understanding by the entire founding generation that the free and independent states were part of a compact of states and did not constitute one consolidated empire. Indeed, they fought a war of secession against just such an empire. To then turn around and create a similar empire of their own would have been thought to be the height of absurdity. The use of the words *United States* in the singular did not become acceptable until after 1865, when the voluntary union of the states was overthrown by a bloody and violent revolution.

After Jefferson's death in 1825, his states' rights tradition was carried on effectively for a quarter of a century most forcefully by John C. Calhoun, who served as vice president of the United States, secretary of war, and U.S. senator from South Carolina. His book, *A Disquisition on Government,* is one of the most insightful political treatises ever written by an American.

Calhoun agreed that a written constitution was desirable (as opposed to Britain's unwritten constitution), but he correctly predicted that those who favored its enforcement would eventually be overpowered, politically, by the "party of government." "At first they [the strict constructionists] might command some respect, and do something to stay the encroachment," he wrote, "but they would, in the progress of the contest, be regarded as mere abstractionists; and, indeed, deservedly, if they should indulge in the folly of supposing that the party in possession of the ballot box and the physical force of the country, could be successfully resisted by an appeal to reason, truth, justice, or the obligations imposed by the constitution. . . . The end of the contest would be the subversion of the constitution."[4] Calhoun forecast that all of the constitutional restrictions on government would ultimately be effectively annulled or ignored and the government would be converted into one of "unlimited powers." He was certainly right. Calhoun, like Jefferson, believed that it was essential for the citizens of the states to possess a "negative power" over the central government, such as the power to decide whether federal laws are constitutional or not. His famous proposal for a "concurrent majority" was designed to allow the citizens of particular states to make these types of decisions since they were, after all, sovereign; the federal government was the citizens' agent or servant prior to 1865, not their master.

## THE JEFFERSONIAN CONSTITUTION

The Jeffersonians' states' rights view of the Constitution prevailed until 1865. The best presentation of this position is St. George Tucker's book, *View of the Constitution of the United States*. Tucker was the professor of law at William and Mary College who took the place of Thomas Jefferson's (and John Marshall's) teacher, George Wythe (a signer of the Declaration of Independence), when Wythe retired.[5] Tucker served with distinction in the American Revolution, where he was wounded in battle; became a successful lawyer afterward; adopted a young John Randolph when he married his widowed mother; and authored one of the first plans for the abolition of slavery in Virginia in 1796.

Tucker warned that any confederacy of states would become a despotism if the central government ever ceased being merely the agent of the states that created it. "The union of the SOV-

EREIGNTY of a state with the [central] government," he wrote, "constitutes a state of USURPATION and absolute TYRANNY, over the people."[6] Moreover, if the "unlimited authority" of the central state were ever to extend so far as to "change the constitution itself, the government, whatever be its form, is absolute and despotic. . . ."[7] Tucker was obviously anticipating what modern-day conservatives bemoan as "judicial activism," another legacy of Lincoln's war.

It was not just the system of checks and balances that was intended to protect the people from tyranny, Tucker explained. It was also "the nature and extent of those powers which the people have reserved to themselves as the Sovereign."[8] Freedom depended crucially on states' rights and divided sovereignty.

Furthermore, Tucker believed that the "doctrine of non-resistance against arbitrary power and oppression" as exercised by a central government "is absurd, slavish, and destructive to the good and happiness of mankind."[9] Having been created by the citizens

To Jeffersonians, states' rights was the most important principle of the U.S. Constitution.

of the states, a free government must be bound to the Constitution "by its creators, the several states in the union, and the citizens thereof." Otherwise, despotism and arbitrary tyranny are inevitable, Tucker warned. And he was right.

Tucker's contemporary John Taylor, a U.S. senator from Virginia, was another Jeffersonian who mocked the idea that the founders would have entrusted the U.S. Supreme Court to be the sole judge of constitutionality and, subsequently, of the limits of the government's own powers. "Being an essential principle for preserving liberty," Taylor wrote in *Tyranny Unmasked,* the Constitution "never could have designed to destroy it, by investing five or six men, installed for life, with a power of

regulating the constitutional rights of all political depart-
ments."[10] After fighting a bloody revolution and creating a new
government that would hopefully protect Americans' natural
rights to life, liberty, and property, the notion that these same
men would then turn around and entrust everyone's liberty to
five or six politically appointed lawyers was a sheer absurdity to
Taylor and to other Jeffersonians.

## STATES' RIGHTS VERSUS TYRANNY DURING
## THE TWENTIETH CENTURY

States' rights might have been essentially destroyed by Lincoln's
war, but no war can eliminate ideas from the minds of the people completely. Though many contemporary conservatives and
libertarians do not seem to appreciate the importance of state
sovereignty in the original federal system, quite a few prominent Jeffersonian scholars during the twentieth century did.
One such scholar was Frank Chodorov, onetime editor of the
magazine *The Freeman* and an icon of the "Old Right." In his
book *The Income Tax: Root of All Evil,* Chodorov wrote that "The
real obstacle [to tyranny] is the psychological resistance to centralization that the States' rights tradition fosters. The citizen
of divided allegiance cannot be reduced to subservience; if
he is in the habit of serving two political gods he cannot
be dominated by either one. . . . No political authority ever
achieved absolutism until the people were deprived of a choice
of loyalties."[11] It was not by accident that Stalin, Mussolini, and
Lenin liquidated any and all competing authorities, Chodorov
noted, before consolidating their power.

To Chodorov dual sovereignty, or what he called "divided authority," was nothing less than "the bulwark of freedom" for
freedom means "the absence of restraint." And "government

cannot give freedom, it can only take it away. The more power the government exercises the less freedom will the people enjoy. And when government has a monopoly of power the people have no freedom. That is the definition of absolutism—monopoly of power."

Americans who wish to understand their history should take heed of this statement in light of the fact that, after the conclusion of Lincoln's war, the Republican Party enjoyed a virtual monopoly of power for almost fifty years. Even when the one non-Republican, Grover Cleveland, was president, Republican policies prevailed.

> All of the worst tyrants of the twentieth century were committed enemies of "divided sovereignty," otherwise known as federalism or states' rights.

The free-market Austrian economist Ludwig von Mises, teacher of Nobel laureate Friedrich A. Hayek (author of the infamous book *The Road to Serfdom*), is another writer who, in the age-old Jeffersonian tradition, understood the importance of states' rights to freedom. Commenting on the effects of government interventionism that was spawned in the United States in the post-1865 era, and in Switzerland during the same period, Mises wrote in *Omnipotent Government*:

> New powers accrued not to the member states but to the federal government. Every step toward more government interference and toward more planning means at the same time an expansion of the jurisdiction of the central government. Washington and Berne were once the seats of the federal governments; today they are capitals in the true sense of the word, and the states and cantons are virtually reduced to the status of provinces. *It is a very significant fact that the adversaries of the trend toward more government control describe*

*their opposition as a fight against Washington and against Berne,*
*i.e., against centralization. It is conceived as a contest of states'*
*rights versus the central power* (emphasis added).[12]

When Mises says that Washington and Berne were once the
seats of the "federal" governments, he meant "federal" in the
true sense of the word, namely, governments that were characterized by divided sovereignty, with states' rights intact. These
cities were merely the "seats" of the central governments that
were created as agents of the free, independent, and sovereign
states and cantons.

To Ludwig von Mises, the fight against governmental
tyranny was fundamentally a fight against consolidated or monopoly government, exactly the kind of government that has
existed in the United States since the late nineteenth century.
This was also a theme of Hayek's *Road to Serfdom,* and of another
Old Right classic, Felix Morley's *Freedom and Federalism.* Morley
was the editor of *National Review* magazine for many years, and
wrote that "Socialism and federalism [i.e., states' rights] are necessarily political opposites because the former demands that
centralized concentration of power which the latter by definition denies."[13]

Economist Murray Rothbard was known before his death in
1995 as the "dean" of the free-market Austrian School of Economics. A student of Mises, he was once labeled "Mr. Libertarian" by *Forbes* magazine. As a young man barely out of college he
wrote a May 11, 1949, letter to the headquarters of the States'
Rights Party in Jackson, Mississippi, that read: "Although a New
Yorker born and bred, I was a staunch supporter of the [Strom]
Thurmond movement." But the problem with the Thurmond
movement was that it was far too narrow, focusing excessively
on what Rothbard called the "Civil Tyranny Program." This pro-

gram of federal "civil rights" regulation should be opposed, Rothbard said, "as an affront to property rights and freedom of association." What was really needed was a national, as opposed to a regional, party to fight "the power hungry Washington bureaucracy."[14]

Rothbard understood that all the talk coming out of Washington at the time of giving greater "civil rights" to minorities was primarily, if not exclusively, motivated more by a hunger for power and money on the part of the Washington bureaucracy than by a concern for justice or humanitarianism. Indeed, when has justice and humanitarianism *ever* been the primary motivator of *any* government?

In addition to these writers, others, such as Nobel laureate economist James M. Buchanan, have also discussed how true federalism is talked about in political circles, but is essentially a dead letter absent the states' rights of nullification and secession.

In contrast, all of the worst tyrants of the past 150 years have been sworn enemies of states' rights and divided sovereignty. Adolf Hitler mocked what he referred to as the "so-called sovereign states" of Germany in *Mein Kampf*.[15] He condemned their "impotence" and "fragmentation" and lavishly praised Otto von Bismarck for all but abolishing states' rights in Germany. This was supposedly a victory in the "struggle between federalism and centralization."[16] Like his nemesis Ludwig von Mises, who fled Austria for America at the outset of World War II hours before the Gestapo broke into his Vienna apartment, Hitler understood that the chief roadblock in the "struggle" for totalitarian socialism (whether it's called

> Vesting too much power in the central government has always been a recipe for tyranny and despotism.

Nazism, communism, fascism, etc.) was federalism, states' rights, and divided sovereignty.

To Hitler the complete abolition of states' rights was essential for the establishment of "a powerful national Reich."[17] Indeed, an earlier generation of German statesmen created this governmental "fragmentation" for the same reasons the American founding fathers created their brand of federalism: to limit the despotic proclivities of any centralized and monopolistic German state.

To make his case against states' rights in *Mein Kampf* Hitler quite logically turned to Abraham Lincoln's first inaugural address for intellectual ammunition. "The individual states of the American Union," the future führer wrote, "could not have possessed any state sovereignty of their own. For it was not these states that formed the Union, on the contrary it was the Union which formed a great part of the so-called states."[18]

This is Hitler's rendition of the false theory of the American founding that Lincoln himself espoused in his first inaugural address. In Lincoln's own words:

> The Union is much older than the Constitution. It was formed, in fact, by the Articles of Association in 1774. It was matured and continued by the Declaration of Independence in 1776. It was further matured . . . by the Articles of Confederation in 1778. And, finally, in 1787, one of the declared objects for ordaining and establishing the Constitution was "to form a more perfect Union."[19]

This statement was as ahistorical as it was logically absurd. It is impossible for the union of two things to be older than either of its parts. That would be akin to saying a marriage can be older than either spouse. In addition, the Union was formed *by the states!* It doesn't matter whether one starts with Lincoln's arbitrarily chosen year of 1774, or the year the Constitution was ratified (1789). The states created the federal Union by retaining their sovereignty and merely delegating certain powers to a central government *for their own mutual benefit.* That is, at least, what they hoped.

Hitler recognized that his dream of omnipotent governmental power under his control could be thwarted by "the struggle between federalism and centralization,"[20] the former of which he blamed on "the Jews." He promised that "The National Socialists [Nazis] . . . would totally eliminate states' rights altogether: Since for us the state as such is only a form,

> Adolf Hitler invoked Lincoln's first inaugural address to make *his* case against state sovereignty in Germany.

but the essential is its content, the nation, the people, it is clear that everything else must be subordinated to its sovereign interests. In particular we cannot grant to any individual state within the nation and the state representing it state sovereignty and sovereignty in point of political power."[21] The "mischief of individual federated states . . . must cease and will some day cease," the aspiring dictator promised. And, "the lesson for the future" is that "the importance of the individual states will in the future no longer lie in the fields of state power and policy."[22]

To Adolf Hitler the essence of Nazism was an omnipotent central government that would rule in the name of "the whole people" or "the whole Arian race" once all aspects of state sovereignty were abolished.

> National Socialism as a matter of principle, must lay claim to the right to force its principles on the whole German nation without consideration of previous federated state

boundaries, and to educate in its ideas and conceptions. Just as the churches do not feel bound and limited by political boundaries, no more does the National Socialist idea feel limited by the individual state territories of our fatherland. The National Socialist doctrine is not the servant of individual federated states, but shall some day become the master of the German nation. It must determine and reorder the life of a people, and must, therefore, imperiously claim the right to pass over [state] boundaries drawn by a development we have rejected.[23]

In his 1962 book *Patriotic Gore,* the literary critic Edmund Wilson noted that Lincoln also had much in common with two other uncompromising enemies of federalism and divided sovereignty during the nineteenth and early twentieth centuries, Lenin and Bismarck.

[I]f we would grasp the significance of the Civil War in relation to the history of our time, we should consider Abraham Lincoln in connection with the other leaders who have been engaged in similar tasks. The chief of these leaders have been Bismarck and Lenin. They with Lincoln have presided over the unifications of the three great new modern powers. . . . Each established a strong central government over hitherto loosely coordinated peoples. Lincoln kept the Union together by subordinating the South to the North; Bismarck imposed on the German states the cohesive hegemony of Prussia; Lenin . . . began the work of binding Russia . . . in a tight bureaucratic net.[24]

Each of these men, wrote Wilson, was an "uncompromising dictator" while in office who was succeeded by newly formed government bureaucracies that became so powerful that "all the bad potentialities of the policies [they] had initiated were realized after [their] removal, in the most undesirable ways."[25]

The lesson here is that constitutional liberty is an empty slogan unless the people remain sovereign, and the only practical way for them to do so is through political communities at the state and local levels, as long as a central government exists. They must also enjoy the rights of nullification and secession, the latter of which has been most important to achieving the amazing rise of freedom in the former Soviet empire in recent years. Fortunately for the Russian people, when the Soviet empire began to crumble and fifteen states (or "republics") decided to secede, Mikhail Gorbachev let them go in peace.

Unlike the communist dictator, Abraham Lincoln refused to negotiate—or even discuss—a separation after the seven states of the lower South seceded. Instead, he launched an invasion and reintroduced total war to the world, resulting in the death of more than six hundred thousand Americans, all to secure a Northern territorial and political monopoly, cleverly disguised by the fanciful and misleading rhetoric of "saving the Union."

# 9

## Lincoln's Big Lie

Another key element of Lincoln's argument against state sovereignty was an argument that he borrowed from Daniel Webster: that the Constitution was created by "the whole people" and not the citizens of the free and independent states. If this were true, said Lincoln, then only "the whole people" could decide to dissolve the Union, not individual states. He asserted that state sovereignty never existed; and that the states were never free and independent of the central government, or, in other words, "the whole people." He enunciated this view in his first inaugural address, and elsewhere. But as James J. Kilpatrick remarked in his book *The Sovereign States,* "The delusion that sovereignty is vested in the whole people of the United States is one of the strangest misconceptions of our public life."[1]

Modern-day proponents of nationalism and executive power still make this argument, however, by pointing to the preamble of the Constitution, which reads, "We the people of the United States . . . do ordain and establish this Constitution. . . ." However, James Madison's *Notes of the Debates in the Federal Convention,* the only written record of the constitutional convention's proceedings, dispels this myth. The preamble of the *first draft* of the U.S. Constitution read:

> We the people of the States of New Hampshire, Massachu-
> setts, Rhode Island and Providence Plantations, Connecticut,
> New-York, New Jersey, Pennsylvania, Delaware, Maryland,
> Virginia, North-Carolina, South Carolina, and Georgia, do or-
> dain, declare, and establish the following Constitution for the
> Government of Ourselves and our Posterity.

Once the founders realized that all the states might not rat-
ify the document—at least not after a considerable amount of
time had passed—the preamble was changed so that the individual states were not named. A state could hardly be named in
the document before the document was actually ratified by that
state. Clearly, the founders never intended one big national act
of ratification by "the whole people." This is a pure fabrication,
invented out of thin air by Daniel Webster, and repeated by
Lincoln decades later to rationalize waging war on the South
and the destruction of the federal system of government created by the founders.

James Madison himself was meticulous in explaining exactly how the ratification of the Constitution was to take
place, for it would determine where sovereignty resided. In his
*Notes* he clearly wrote that the Constitution would be ratified
by "the people composing those political societies [of the
states], in their highest sovereign capacity." It was *not* state
governments that possessed this power, moreover, but *the citizens of the states.* The people *delegated* certain powers to their
elected representatives, but retained ultimate sovereignty to
themselves, as members of separate political communities
called states.

The national government was created by the process whereby state ratifying conventions chose to delegate certain powers, previously delegated to the states, to the central government. For example, under the Articles of Confederation the central government had no taxing powers of its own, but it was able to impose tariffs and excise taxes under the Constitution.

Lincoln's assertion in the Gettysburg Address that "a new nation" was created in 1776 (four score and seven years prior to 1863) was wrong on all counts. The founders never created "a nation" but a confederacy of states. And the Declaration of Independence never had the legal authority of either the Articles of Confederation or the Constitution. More important, the very words of the Declaration contradict Lincoln's theory of the absence of state sovereignty. The Declaration was, first and foremost, a *Declaration of Secession* from the British Empire. America was founded by a War of Secession. "Secession" means a separation from a community of one part of that community, according to *Black's Law Dictionary*. This is surely what the Revolution of 1776 was all about. The founders could hardly have thought that secession was an illegitimate act when it was what defined *them* politically. They were all secessionists, to the man. It was the "loyalists," such as Benedict Arnold, who were the antisecessionists and traitors.

> The founding fathers understood that the states were sovereign. Lincoln "proved" them wrong at gunpoint.

The concluding paragraph of the Declaration of Independence announced to the world that the colonists were seceding from the British Empire as citizens of free and independent states, not as "the whole people." As the Declaration states: "These colonies are, and of Right ought to be Free and Independent States, they have full power to levy War, conclude Peace, contract Alliances, establish commerce, and to do all other Acts and things which Independent States may of right do." Clearly, the founders viewed the individual states as, essentially, separate *countries,* each of which was to even have the right to wage war. Indeed, by the time war broke out in 1861, it was quite common for such figures as Robert E. Lee to refer to their home states as "my country."

When the Revolution ended, the king of England did not sign a peace treaty with something called "The United States of America," in the singular. Article I of the *Treaty with Great Britain* that ended the American Revolution states:

> His Britannic Majesty acknowledges the said United States, vis, New Hampshire, Massachusetts Bay, Rhode Island, and Providence Plantations, Connecticut, New York, New Jersey, Pennsylvania, Delaware, Maryland, Virginia, North Carolina, South Carolina, and Georgia to be free, sovereign and independent States; that he treats with them as such and for himself, his heirs and successors, Relinquishes all claims to the Government, proprietary and territorial rights of the Same, and every part thereof.

When the citizens of the states created a federal constitution in the form of the Articles of Confederation, they made a point of clearly spelling out their independent and sovereign status. As defined in Article I, Section II: "Each State retains its sovereignty, freedom and independence, and every power, jurisdiction and right, which is not by this confederation expressly delegated to the United States, in Congress assembled." Sovereignty always rested in the hands of the citizens of the states, never with "the whole people."

In *Federalist #39,* James Madison, the "father of the Constitution,"

rejected what would become Lincoln's Big Lie regarding the
founding of the Republic. The Constitution was to be ratified
by the people "not as individuals composing one entire nation,
but as composing the distinct and independent States to which
they respectively belong." He
also stated the new government created by the Constitution got *all* of its authority
from the citizens of the free
and independent states, and that each state involved in ratifying the Constitution was "considered as a sovereign body,
independent of all others, and only to be bound by its own
voluntary act." Lincoln disagreed; he believed that the states
should be bound together at the barrel of a gun or cannon, if
necessary.

"The whole people" had nothing
whatsoever to do with the
adoption of the Constitution.

The "whole people," in other words, had nothing whatsoever
to do with the formation of the government. Either Lincoln
never read the *Federalist Papers,* which is likely, or he lied about
their contents in his political speeches.

The primary documents that chronicle this country's founding are at odds with Lincoln's anti-state-sovereignty theory. The
phrase "United States" is always in the plural in the Constitution and all the other founding documents, signifying not one
consolidated government, but a confederacy of states. The president is not elected by "the whole people" but by an electoral
college that consists of appointees from each state, chosen by
state legislatures. Until 1914, U.S. senators were appointed
by state legislatures and not popularly elected. The reason for
this, once again, was to assure state sovereignty over the central
government. Prior to the Seventeenth Amendment, passed in
1913, a number of state legislatures actually recalled and re-

placed their U.S. senators for acting against the interests of the citizens of their own states upon arriving in Washington.[2] No new state may be formed, according to the Constitution, "within the Jurisdiction of any other state; nor any State be formed by the Junction of two or more States, or Parts of States, without the Consent of the Legislatures of the States concerned as well as Congress." This ensures state control over the creation of new states and was one of many constitutional provisions that Lincoln discarded when he orchestrated the illegal secession of West Virginia from the rest of Virginia. Amending the Constitution still requires ratification by three-fourths of the states, not a popular vote of "the whole people."

The founders feared mass democracy or rule by "the whole people." This is why they attempted to carefully limit the abilities of the central government, with the states delegating only seventeen very specific responsibilities (in Article I, Section 8 of the U.S. Constitution). It is also why they created the system of checks and balances and the whole edifice of dual sovereignty or federalism. Lincoln denied all of this, invented a new theory of the founding, and waged the bloodiest war in world history up to that point to "prove" himself right.

As long as this nationalist myth prevails the American people can never regain true sovereignty over their government. It is no surprise that contemporary advocates of more-or-less dictatorial executive branch powers and military aggression (i.e., the "neoconservatives") invoke the Lincoln legend time and again to "justify" the interventionist policies that they pursue. It worked for Lincoln, and his political descendants have relied on it ever since.

# 10

A "Great Crime":
The Arrest Warrant for the Chief Justice
of the United States

Imagine that in 2006 America had a chief justice of the
United States who firmly believed in enforcing the Constitution and issued an opinion that the war in Iraq was unconstitutional because Congress did not fulfill its constitutional duty in
declaring war. Imagine also that the administration and its allies
in the media responded with a vicious propaganda campaign
that demonized the chief justice as unpatriotic, and possibly
even treasonous. Imagine that this media campaign then emboldened the American president who launched the war to issue
an arrest warrant for the chief justice, effectively destroying the
constitutional separation of powers and establishing a de facto
dictatorship.

This sequence of events actually happened during the early
Lincoln administration. Abraham Lincoln issued an arrest warrant for Chief Justice Roger B. Taney after the eighty-four-year-
old jurist issued an opinion that only Congress, and not the
president, can legally suspend the writ of habeas corpus. Taney's
opinion, issued as part of his duties as a circuit court judge (a
duty that Supreme Court justices had in those days), relied on

the case of *Ex Parte Merryman* (May 1861). The essence of his opinion was not that habeas corpus could never be suspended under the Constitution, only that the document requires Congress to do it, not the president. In other words, if it was truly in the "public interest" to suspend due process (a dubious assumption at any time), then the representatives of the people should have no problem doing so. The Lincoln administration could have appealed the chief justice's ruling, but it chose to simply ignore it and, worse yet, to intimidate the elderly judge by issuing an arrest warrant for him.

Several sources corroborate the story that Lincoln actually issued an arrest warrant for the chief justice, a breathtaking act of despotism. The warrant was never served for lack of a federal marshal with the nerve to drag the elderly chief justice out of his chambers and throw him into the dungeonlike military prison at Fort McHenry in Baltimore.

> Rather than appealing an unfavorable opinion by the chief justice of the United States, Lincoln issued an arrest warrant for the elderly judge.

The first source of the story is a history of the U.S. Marshal's Service written by Frederick S. Calhoun, the chief historian for the Service, entitled *The Lawmen: United States Marshals and Their Deputies, 1789–1989*. Calhoun recounts the words of Lincoln's former law partner, Ward Hill Lamon, who also served in the Lincoln administration, and matter-of-factly mentioned the arrest warrant in a book that he wrote after the war. Lamon's account of Lincoln's arrest warrant for the chief justice is discussed in a chapter of Calhoun's book entitled "Arrest of Traitors and Suspension of Habeas Corpus."

Upon hearing of Lamon's verification of the Taney arrest story, the Lincoln cult immediately began claiming that Lamon was a drunkard whose word could not be trusted, despite the fact that Lincoln himself obviously trusted him, employing him as a close adviser. Ulysses S. Grant was another notorious drunkard of the era, but somehow the Lincoln cult never doubts anything he said or wrote.

Unfortunately for the Lincoln cult, there are several more very reliable accounts of the arrest warrant. One of them is an 1887 book by George W. Brown, the wartime mayor of Baltimore, entitled *Baltimore and the Nineteenth of April, 1861: A Study of War.* In it is the transcript of a conversation Mayor Brown had with Taney in which Judge Taney mentions his knowledge that Lincoln had issued an arrest warrant for him.

Yet another corroborating source is *A Memoir of Benjamin Robbins Curtis,* a former U.S. Supreme Court justice. Judge Curtis represented President Andrew Johnson in his impeachment trial before the U.S. Senate; wrote the dissenting opinion in the *Dred Scott* case; and resigned from the Supreme Court over a dispute with Judge Taney over that case. Nevertheless, in his memoirs he praises the propriety of Justice Taney in upholding the Constitution by opposing Lincoln's unilateral suspension of habeas corpus. He refers to the arrest warrant for the chief justice, accusing him of treason, as "a great crime."

> Judge Benjamin Robbins Curtis, who wrote the dissenting opinion in the *Dred Scott* case, thought Lincoln's arrest warrant for the chief justice was "a great crime."

There is also growing evidence that intimidation of federal judges was a common practice of the Lincoln administration. In October 1861 Lincoln ordered the District of Columbia provost marshal to place armed sentries around the home of a Washington, D.C., circuit court judge and place him under house arrest. The reason for the arrest: the judge had carried out his constitutional duty to issue a writ of habeas corpus to a young man being detained by the provost marshal, allowing the man to have due process. The judge's actions were later vindicated by the U.S. Supreme Court. After the war, the Court ruled that neither the president nor Congress can legally suspend habeas corpus as long as the civil courts are operating, as they certainly were in the Northern states in 1861.

By placing the judge under house arrest Lincoln prevented him from attending the hearing in the case.[1] The latter ruling contained a letter from Judge W. M. Merrick, the judge of the Circuit Court of the District of Columbia, explaining how, after issuing the writ of habeas corpus to the young man, he was placed under house arrest. Here's the final paragraph of the letter:

> After dinner I visited my brother judges in Georgetown, and returning home between half past seven and eight o'clock found an armed sentinel stationed at my door by order of the Provost-Marshal. I learned that this guard had been placed at my door as early as five o'clock. Armed sentries from that time continuously until now have been stationed in front of my house. Thus it appears that a military officer against whom a writ in the appointed form of law has first threatened with and afterwards arrested and imprisoned the attorney who rightfully served the writ upon him. He continued, and still continues, in contempt and disregard of the mandate of the law, and has ignominiously placed an armed guard to insult and intimidate by its presence the Judge who ordered the writ to issue, and still keeps up this armed array at his door, in defiance and contempt of the justice of the land. Under the circumstances I respectfully request the Chief Judge of the Circuit Court to cause this

memorandum to be read in open Court, to show the reasons
for my absence from my place upon the bench, and that he
will cause this paper to be entered at length on the minutes
of the Court.

W. M. Merrick
Assistant Judge of the Circuit Court
of the District of Columbia

The Lincoln cult has an excuse for everything, and in this
case the party line is that federal judges were imprisoned by federal marshals, not Lincoln himself. But that's like saying that
Lincoln was not responsible for any of the battlefield deaths
during the war because he did not personally pull the trigger of a
gun to shoot someone despite the fact that he was the commander in chief. Thus, according to the cultists Lincoln would have
had to personally hold federal judges prisoner at gunpoint to be
considered involved in the arrest.

But Lincoln himself was fully aware that this was going on
and did nothing to stop it. The reason he did nothing, obviously,
was that it was his intended policy.

The implications of the arrest warrant for Judge Taney are
that the separation of powers was essentially destroyed, along
with the place of the Supreme Court in the constitutional
scheme of American government. It essentially made executive
power supreme, over all others, and put the president, the military, and the executive branch of government in control of
American society.

# PART II

# Economic Issues You're Supposed to Ignore

# 11

## The Origins of the Republican Party

When the Whig Party imploded in the early 1850s Abraham Lincoln assured the people of Illinois that there were very few differences, if any, between the old Whig and the new Republican Party he had just joined. The Whig Party was always the party of government interventionism, with its "American System" of protectionist tariffs, corporate welfare for road-, canal-, and railroad-building corporations, and a federal government bank to help finance all of these dubious schemes.

This time Lincoln was not lying to the American people. Sure enough, as soon as the newly created Republican Party gained enough power to influence national legislation, it picked up right where the Whig Party had left off. The Republicans forced the U.S. House of Representatives to pass the protectionist Morrill Tariff bill during the 1859–60 session of Congress — before Lincoln's election and before any Southern state had seceded. This fact is important because it shows that the high tariff policy was *the top priority* of the Republican Party and not just a mechanism for financing the war. The moment the party gained enough power to pass legislation, the piece of legislation that was at the top of its list of priorities was a high, protection-ist tariff that would "protect" mostly Northern manufacturers from international competition. It was a protectionist tariff, not a war-financing tariff.

One of the first legislative successes of the new Republican Party was to more than double the average tariff rate.

The party then defended Southern slavery by explicitly defending the institution in its 1860 party platform, and by overwhelmingly support-ing a proposed constitutional amendment that would have prohibited the federal government from ever interfering with Southern slavery.

Even when the Republicans did oppose the extension of slavery into the new territories, it was motivated much more by politics and economics than by humanitarianism. In fact, Lincoln and other party leaders explicitly stated that they wanted to preserve the territories for the white race. Even Pennsylvania congressman David Wilmot's famous proviso (a law first introduced in Congress—but never passed—in 1846 that would have barred slavery from the new territories ac-quired by the Mexican War) was referred to by Wilmot himself as "the white man's proviso." The reason he and other North-ern politicians gave for wanting to ban slavery in the terri-tory acquired by the Mexican War was not that they wanted to strike a blow against slavery, but that they did not want any black people—free or slave—living among them. Lincoln himself was very explicit about this. As historian Eugene Berwanger explained in *The Frontier Against Slavery*: "Republi-cans made no pretense of being concerned with the fate of the Negro and insisted that theirs was a party of white labor. By in-troducing a note of white supremacy, they hoped to win the votes of the Negrophobes and the anti-abolitionists who were opposed to the extension of slavery."[1]

To the early Republicans "free soil" meant more than free land giveaways by the federal government; it also meant soil that was free of black people. The Republican Party championed the free giveaway of land to settlers in the territories and also catered to the almost unanimous Northern preference that the territories remain as free as possible of black people, free or slave. In other words, they wanted the territories to look like New England. (Southern Democrats favored *selling* the land to settlers in order to raise revenue for the government that would take pressure off of the tariff as the government's main source of revenue. The South was an agrarian society that exported as much as three-fourths of everything it produced. Since protectionist tariffs tend to diminish the overall amount of international trade, they saw protectionism as virtually all cost and no benefit to them, just the opposite of the viewpoint of the North where manufacturing was more prevalent.)

A second reason given for opposing the extension of slavery was to continue skewing the balance of political power in Congress in favor of the North. Because of the Three-Fifths Clause of the Constitution that existed at the time, every five slaves counted as three persons for purposes of determining the number of congressional representatives within each state. Lincoln himself clearly stated that he was opposed to slavery extension precisely because it would artificially inflate the congressional representation of the Democratic Party. If this came to pass, then the old Whig economic agenda of protectionist tariffs, corporate welfare, and central banking, which had become the Republican agenda, would continue to fail in Congress.

Some of the most renowned Lincoln biographers fail to understand the meaning and importance of these economic issues, and for good reason: They are historians, not economists. An example is an essay in the October 2004 issue of *The Smithsonian* magazine by Pulitzer Prize–winning Lincoln biographer David Donald. The essay, entitled "The Road Not Taken," was part of a symposium that posed the question of what America would look like today if the presidential elections of 1860, 1912, 1932, and 1980 had turned out differently. Donald focused on the Lincoln administration's "social legislation" and concluded that, had Lincoln not been elected in 1860, a Democratic majority in Congress

> would have blocked the important economic and social legislation enacted by the Republicans during the Civil War. Thus, there would likely have been no high tariff laws that protected the iron industry, so essential in postwar economic development, no Homestead Act giving 160 acres to settlers willing to occupy and till land out West, no transcontinental railroad legislation, no land-grant colleges, no currency or national banking system, no Department of Agriculture to offer expert guidance on better seeds and improved tillage. Without such legislation, the economic takeoff that made the United States a major industrial power by the end of the century would have been prevented.

The Lincoln cult is hopelessly confused when it comes to economic policy issues, especially the tariff.

It is not clear that Southern Democrats would have been able to block this legislation—the population of the North had been rapidly outstripping that of the South, leading to greater congressional representation in the former region. And there were about twice as many U.S. senators from Northern states as there were from the states that seceded. But aside from that point, every single one of these sentences is false. Protectionist tariffs made the iron industry lazy and inefficient, which is always the case when any industry is isolated from competitive pressures. The industry did develop, but it would have developed faster and more efficiently without protectionism. Moreover, the high-priced steel caused by Lincoln-era tariffs (which lasted for over half a century) was a hindrance to all steel-using industries in America and hobbled their development. Everything made in America of steel was more costly to manufacture due to Republican Party protectionism. This rendered American manufacturing much less competitive on international markets during that period. American manufacturing industry developed *despite* this economic roadblock, not because of it. In addition, America's trade partners abroad retaliated to some degree with high tariffs of their own on American-made goods imported into their countries. This constituted a second dose of economic harm to American industry thanks to Republican Party protectionism. David Donald got it all backwards.

The effect of Republican Party protectionism was to make the iron and steel industry inefficient, which caused it to become a perennial whiner and complainer and beggar for more protection from competition. Indeed, one of the first things President George W. Bush did upon taking office in 2001 was to impose 50 percent tariffs on imported steel. How long will this industry claim to be an "infant industry" in need of protection from competition? American consumers were plundered by all of this protectionism, which reduced their standard of living by forcing them to pay more for all goods that were made with steel.

Late-nineteenth-century protectionist tariffs were especially harmful to American farmers who had to purchase expensive farm tools and machinery made of steel. Also, by restricting international trade, protectionism reduced the wealth of our foreign trading partners, who in turn purchased fewer American goods, especially farm goods, an area where the United States has long had a comparative advantage. Thus, American farmers were hurt twice by Lincolnian protectionism: once by having to purchase higher-priced farm tools and machinery, and again by the reduction in American agricultural exports.

As for the Homestead Act, historian Ludwell Johnson long ago determined that the majority of the land was not given to individual settlers but to mining, timber, and railroad corporations.[2] As is always the case with subsidies to corporations, there was a colossal amount of corruption, especially with regard to the land giveaways associated with the government-subsidized transcontinental railroads.

Giving the land away for free (or for a pittance) made the Republican Party, which controlled the federal government for decades after the war, very popular, but it also increased pressures to keep tariff rates high in an era where there was no income tax. It was therefore a win/win policy for the Republicans, but lose/lose for the rest of society: It was a way of indirectly "buying" votes and campaign contributions from settlers and corporations who were given free land, while supporting its protectionist trade policy and cementing the political support of Northern industry.

The government-subsidized transcontinental railroads, which Donald also praises, were arguably the worst example in American history of the corruption and inefficiency that is associated with massive government "public works" projects. They resulted in the Credit Mobilier scandal of the Grant administration. Entrepreneur James J. Hill proved that the subsidies were unnecessary by building a nonsubsidized transcontinental railroad, the Great Northern, which was constructed and operated much more efficiently than the scandal-prone government-subsidized railroads.

Land grant colleges have also been a mixed blessing, as government money inevitably led to greater government control of higher education, culminating with today's plague of "political correctness" on college campuses and in much of the rest of society. It has also led to the politicization of scientific research and the creation of academics who are essentially "hired guns" for the various government agencies that fund their research and, at times, pay their salaries.[3]

Donald's assertion that federal government bureaucrats were necessary to educate farmers about what kinds of seeds to plant seems absurd. At best, such government programs are simply a means of getting American taxpayers to pay for things that farmers—who *are* businessmen after all—should be paying for themselves. There's no need for a U.S. Department of Automobiles to instruct automobile manufacturers on what kinds of tires and engine parts to use in their cars any more than there is a need for a U.S. Department of Agriculture to instruct farmers on what seeds to plant. The private sector can and does do a much better job of making those decisions.

In addition to providing unnecessary subsidies to mostly large corporate farms, the U.S. Department of Agriculture has made agricultural markets grotesquely inefficient. It has done this through various programs that pay farmers for *not* growing food or raising livestock, only to allow farmers to charge higher prices and make more money; price control programs that prop up food prices above free-market levels, causing large surpluses that often go to waste; and hooking millions of farmers on government debt that they will never be able to pay off.[4]

Donald's praise for Lincoln's National Currency Acts is also misplaced (to be discussed in more detail in Chapter 15). These acts immediately created unprecedented rates of inflation during the war and ushered in a much more unstable banking system than the one that had preceded it, known as the "Independent Treasury System."

Liberal historians like David Donald and James McPherson praise Lincoln's "social legislation" because to them it appears to be a precursor to Franklin D. Roosevelt's New Deal, and indeed it was. In fact, the phrase "New Deal" was not coined by Roosevelt but by a Raleigh, North Carolina, newspaper in 1865 when describing Lincoln's social legislation. The newspaper urged North Carolinians to rejoin the Union and enjoy the government handouts that had been created by what economists Mark Thornton and Robert Ekelund call "the flurry of new laws, regulations, and bureaucracies created by President Lincoln and the Republican Party."[5] These included the Homestead Act, Morrill Land-Grant College Act, Department of Agriculture, transcontinental railroad land grants, tax-subsidized mail delivery, subsidized railway mail service, and other programs, all financed by myriad excise taxes, ten tariff increases, and the printing of greenbacks.

The phrase "New Deal" was originally coined to describe the domestic policies of the Lincoln administration.

The Republican Party was always, from its inception, the party of big government in America. It was the Democratic Party that was the party of Jefferson and of limited government, at least until the 1912 election, after which the party veered dramatically to the left. That's why liberal historians like David Donald so often portray the Republican Party's nineteenth-century origins in such a heroic light.

# 12

## The Great Railroad Lobbyist

Senator John Sherman, chairman of the powerful U.S. Senate Finance Committee during the Lincoln administration and brother of General Sherman, explained why the Republican Party nominated and elected Abraham Lincoln: "Those who elected Mr. Lincoln," the senator said, expected him "to secure to free labor its just right to the Territories of the United States; to protect . . . by wise revenue laws, the labor of our people; to secure the public lands to actual settlers . . . ; to develop the internal resources of the country by opening new means of communications between the Atlantic and Pacific."[1]

From the perspective of the Republican Party, Lincoln was elected for four reasons: first, to preserve the territories for the white race and to ensure that white laborers would not have to compete for jobs with either slaves or free blacks; second, to sign into law high protectionist tariffs that would benefit Northern manufacturers while harming all consumers, and especially those in the South; third, to give away free land under a Homestead Act, the biggest political patronage program ever; and fourth, to use taxpayer dollars to subsidize railroad corporations, the important financial backbone of the Republican Party. They decided that Abraham Lincoln—the wealthy, skilled trial lawyer/politician/lobbyist from the railroad industry—was the man for the job.

The Whig Party was always the party of the moneyed elite, and Lincoln was a Whig much longer than he was a Republican. As a member of the Illinois legislature in the 1830s he led his local delegation in a successful Whig Party effort to appropriate some $12 million in taxpayer dollars for subsidies to road-, canal-, and railroad-building corporations. In his book *Lincoln and the Railroads*, first published in 1927, John W. Starr, Jr., noted how one of Lincoln's legislative colleagues in Illinois commented that "he seemed to be a born politician" and so "we followed his lead." Lincoln had grandiose plans, writes Starr. There was to be "a railroad from Galena in the extreme northwestern part of the state"; north of St. Louis "three roads were to radiate"; and "there was also a road to run from Quincy . . . through Springfield" and "another one from Warsaw . . . to Peoria"; and yet another "from Pekin . . . to Bloomington."[2] Unfortunately for Illinois taxpayers, this "leadership" led to a huge financial debacle, with literally *no* projects being completed and all of the money being either wasted or stolen.

The whole mess was a disaster for the state government and the taxpayers, but it was a boon to Lincoln's political and legal careers, catapulting him into position as one of the top railroad industry lobbyists, even before the word *lobbyist* was coined.

By 1860 the Illinois Central Railroad was one of the largest corporations in the world. In a company history (cited by Starr), author J. G. Drennan noted that "Mr. Lincoln was continuously one of the attorneys for the Illinois Central Railroad Company from its organization [in 1849] until he was elected president."[3] He was called upon by the company's general counsel to litigate dozens of cases and was such a corporate insider that he traveled throughout the Midwest in a private rail car with a free pass and was often accompanied by an entourage of Illinois Central executives. This was the real Lincoln, a man diametrically opposed to the false image of the poor, humble, backwoods "railsplitter" that has been presented to generations of American schoolchildren.

In one case Lincoln successfully defended the Illinois Central against McLean County, Illinois, which wanted to tax the corporation's property. After winning the case he sent the company a bill for $5,000, an incredible sum for a single case in the 1850s. The man who Lincoln presented his bill to was George B. McClellan, the vice president of the Illinois Central who later became the commanding general of the Army of the Potomac (until Lincoln fired him) and, in 1864, Lincoln's opponent in the presidential election.

Starr explains an underhanded scheme that was apparently hatched by Lincoln and McClellan to get Lincoln his fee. McClellan initially refused to pay the fee, stating that his New York City board of directors would never condone paying such a hefty sum to an Illinois "country lawyer." Lincoln then sued the Illinois Central for his fee. When he appeared in court, however, armed with depositions from other Illinois lawyers swearing that such a fee seemed perfectly appropriate to them, no lawyers for the company showed up. Lincoln was awarded his exorbitant fee by default.

> Lincoln and his friend General George B. McClellan were consummate railroad industry insiders.

Starr suggests that this whole episode was a ruse used to essentially swindle money out of the company's board of directors, evidenced by the fact that McClellan continued to employ

Lincoln. "Lincoln continued to handle the [Illinois Central's] litigation afterwards, the same as he had done before."[4]

By the late 1850s it was widely known that "Lincoln's close relations with powerful industrial interests" were "always potent and present in political counsels."[5] In today's language, Lincoln was the equivalent of a rich and powerful "K Street lobbyist." In a great understatement, Starr remarked that "Lincoln's rise [in politics] was coincident with that of the railroads."[6]

Indeed, in addition to representing the Illinois Central, Lincoln also represented the Chicago and Alton, Ohio and Mississippi, and Rock Island railroads. As soon as the Chicago and Mississippi Railroad was built, he was appointed the local attorney for that corporation. By 1860 he was probably the most sought-after attorney in the entire industry. He was so prominent that the New York financier Erastus Corning offered him the job of general counsel to the New York Central Railroad at a starting salary of $10,000 a year, a huge salary at the time; he turned down the offer.

> Lincoln was a political tool of rich and powerful corporations. Today he would be called a "lobbyist."

Lincoln's insider status allowed him to engage in some very lucrative real estate speculation. On one of his trips by private rail car to participate in litigation on behalf of the Illinois Central, he and his entourage "decided to go to Council Bluffs, Iowa, where he had some real estate investments."[7] "Shortly before that trip," writes Starr, "Abraham Lincoln had purchased several town lots from his fellow railroad attorney, Norman B. Judd, who had acquired them from the Chicago and Rock Island Railroad." Council Bluffs at that time was a frontier town, containing about fifteen hundred people. To this day, the parcel of land there that once belonged to Abraham Lincoln is called "Lincoln's Hill."

Why did he invest in real estate in Council Bluffs, Iowa, of all places, when he was surely more familiar with Chicago or Springfield, Illinois, which were larger and more rapidly growing cities? A likely reason is that, as a political and industry insider, Lincoln knew there was a high likelihood that the government would eventually subsidize a transcontinental railroad, and that Council Bluffs would be a good starting point for such a railroad. An acquaintance of his, the renowned railroad industry engineer Grenville Dodge, had told him so.

When he took office as president, Lincoln called a special session of Congress in July 1861 to propose "emergency" legislation to create the taxpayer-subsidized Union Pacific Railroad. Time was of the essence, for if the war ended quickly and the Southern Democrats returned to Congress, such a project might not fly. "There was no firmer friend of the Union Pacific bill than the president himself," writes Starr. The bill was passed in 1862 and it gave the president the power to appoint all the directors and commissioners and, more important, it gave him the power "to fix the point of commencement" of the Union Pacific Railroad. Not surprisingly, Lincoln chose Council Bluffs, Iowa, as the eastern terminus of the railroad and, coincidentally, Grenville Dodge became chief engineer for the railroad.

> Lincoln chose Council Bluffs, Iowa, where he had personally invested in real estate, as the eastern terminus for the government-subsidized transcontinental railroad.

The Pacific Railroad bill was a gigantic political payoff to the Northern business interests that supported Lincoln's political career and the Republican

Party. As Dee Brown wrote in his classic history of the transcontinental railroads, *Hear That Lonesome Whistle Blow*, when Lincoln signed the bill he "assured the fortunes of a dynasty of American families . . . the Brewsters, Bushnells, Olcotts, Harkers, Harrisons, Trowbridges, Lanworthys, Reids, Ogdens, Bradfords, Noyeses, Brooks, Cornells, and dozens of others."[8]

Lincoln had been associated with a powerful clique of New England/New York/Chicago businessmen, including Thomas Clark Durant, Peter Day, Grenville Dodge, and Benedict Reed. These men all had experience in canal and railroad building and financing, and when, in 1857, they were looking for a lawyer to represent their Rock Island and Pacific Railroad, they settled on Abraham Lincoln. These men would later go on to fame and fortune as notorious "robber barons" involved in the government-subsidized transcontinental railroad industry after the war.

> Lincoln's cherished Pacific Railroad Bill became the mother of all political payoffs.

In *Hear That Lonesome Whistle Blow* Dee Brown wrote of how this Northern clique of slick political operators and businessmen "aroused the suspicions of the South" when they lobbied for huge sums of tax dollars—paid for in part with Southern taxes—to be allocated by Congress for the building of a transcontinental railroad across *the Northern states.*[9]

Virtually all of the leading lights of the Republican Party were involved in the scheme. John C. Fremont, who would be a general in Lincoln's army, was a wealthy Northern California engineer who conducted an extensive engineering survey "to make certain that the most favorable route would end up not in San Diego but in Northern California" where he owned large land holdings.[10] Congressman Thaddeus Stevens "received a block of [Union Pacific] stock in exchange for his vote" on the Pacific

Railroad bill. He also demanded, as a condition of his "yes" vote, insertion of a clause (in the law) requiring that all iron used in the construction and equipment of said railroad to be American manufacture.[11] Stevens was an iron manufacturer from Pennsylvania. At the time, British steel was cheaper than American steel, and Stevens's "restrictive clause" cost the American taxpayers millions, while likely lining the congressman's pockets very handsomely indeed.

Republican congressman Oakes Ames, "who with his brother Oliver manufactured shovels in Massachusetts, became a loyal ally [of the Union Pacific] and helped to pressure the 1864 Pacific Railway Act through the war-corrupted Congress," Dee Brown wrote.[12] It must have taken *a lot of shovels* to dig railroad beds from Iowa to California.

> Many of the leading lights of the national Republican Party profited very handsomely from the government-subsidized transcontinental railroad.

During the postwar Grant administration, writes Brown, the Republican Speaker of the House of Representatives, Schuyler Colfax (later Grant's vice president), visited the western railroad routes to attend a ceremony in his honor. But he wasn't interested in being honored. "He preferred cash above honors, and back in Washington he eagerly accepted a bundle of Credit Mobilier stock from his fellow congressman Oakes Ames, and thus became a loyal friend of the Union Pacific," says Dee Brown.[13]

Another one of Lincoln's generals, John Dix, "spent most of his time strutting about Washington in a general's uniform," but was in reality the Washington, D.C., lobbyist for the railroads.[14] General Sherman himself was sold land at below-market prices by the railroad, and after the war would conduct a decades-long campaign of ethnic genocide against the Plains Indians, admittedly to make way for the government-subsidized railroads.

After the war Lincoln's old business associate, Grenville Dodge, the railroad's chief engineer, proposed making slaves of the Indians instead of killing them, forcing them "to do the grading, with the Army furnishing a guard to make the Indians work, and keep them from running away."[15] In the end, it was apparently decided to kill as many Indians as possible instead, and place the rest on reservations "where they can be watched," as Sherman once said.

It is not an exaggeration to say that one of the primary reasons—if not *the* primary reason—for the creation of the Republican Party was to establish the largest political patronage program in the history of government. This was always the pipe dream of the old Whigs like Abraham Lincoln, who understood that such a system could cement them in power for generations (which of course it did). This dream was achieved beginning with the government-subsidized transcontinental railroads, and no one was more important and influential in achieving this dubious accomplishment than was Abraham Lincoln, the old railroad industry lobbyist.

# 13

## The Great Protectionist

If there is one thing that creates hysteria among the gate-keepers of the Lincoln legend, it is the suggestion that among the causes of the War between the States were economic issues besides slavery in the territories. Usually, the idea is loudly denounced, sneered at, labeled an "old chestnut" (as it has been by "Civil War" historian William C. Davis),[1] a "red herring," or some other kind of strange plant or animal. Searching through the modern literature of the war, one finds relatively little mention of economic issues despite the fact that North and South were consumed for the previous half century by conflicts over tariffs, banking, internal improvements, land policy, and other economic issues. Both Jefferson Davis and Abraham Lincoln mentioned the tariff issue very prominently in their respective first inaugural addresses. *They* obviously thought it was an important issue of the day. There is a conspiracy of silence over this issue, which should pique the curiosity of any student of American history.[2]

The conspiracy is beginning to crumble, helped by the publication of my book, *The Real Lincoln, When in the Course of Human*

*Events* by Charles Adams, and *Tariffs, Blockades, and Inflation* by Mark Thornton and Robert B. Ekelund. Thornton and Ekelund argue quite forcefully that "economics is necessary to understand the causes, course, and consequences" of the war, and they cite contemporary economic research showing that a major cause of civil wars throughout the world has been conflicts over international trade policy. The American Civil War of 1861–1865 was no different.

## THE FIRST SHOT IN AMERICA'S TARIFF WAR

The great conflict between the limited, decentralized government and free-trade Jeffersonians, and the Hamiltonian champions of a more active, centralized, and protectionist state began manifesting itself in a North-South dispute over tariff policy in the early 1820s. In 1824 Henry Clay sponsored a tariff bill that was passed into law and that approximately doubled the average tariff rate. The agricultural South was immediately alarmed, for it was well understood that protectionist tariffs almost exclusively benefited Northern manufacturers while forcing Southerners to pay more for everything from farm tools to woolen blankets. Very little was manufactured in the South at the time, so there were virtually no benefits to a protectionist tariff. To the South, it was all cost and no benefit. The South would abide by a modest "revenue tariff" of 10–15 percent, just sufficient to pay most of the expenses of running the central government, but not a protectionist tariff designed to thwart international competition. Thus, the region's political leaders saw Henry Clay's Tariff of 1824 as an instrument of plunder and a break with the constitutional contract that called for taxes that were uniform and proportioned to the states according to population.

The breakdown of the vote in Congress on the Tariff of 1824 clearly shows that the boundries of a regional conflict had already been defined. Of the 107 House of Representatives votes in favor of the tariff, only three came from Southern states (2.8 percent of the vote). Sixty-four Southern congressmen voted no. In the U.S. Senate, a mere two of twenty-five yes votes came from Southern states (8 percent of the vote); fourteen Southern senators voted nay.

Emboldened by their success with the tariff increase of 1824, the economic nationalists in Congress, led once again by Lincoln's political idol, Henry Clay, succeeded in increasing the tariff rate even further, to an average rate of almost 50 percent in 1828. This "Tariff of Abominations" was loudly denounced throughout the South, especially in South Carolina, home of the port of Charleston. As recounted in *The Nullification Controversy in South Carolina* by historian Chauncy Boucher, South Carolina's politicians denounced the tariff as a "usurpation" and as a "system of robbery and plunder" which "made one section tributary to another," only so that "corrupt politicians" of the North could "buy up partisans and retain power."[3] They were right, of course.

> The North began plundering the South with protectionist tariffs as early as 1824.

There were a few Southern protectionists and advocates of "internal improvement" spending by government, but in general, the South was adamantly opposed to the whole package of protectionist tariffs, corporate welfare, and central banking that would become the keystone of the Northern-dominated Whig Party for the next twenty-five years and, after that, of the Republican Party. In 1825 the South Carolina legislature adopted a set of resolutions condemning protectionist tariffs, government subsidies to corporations, and a national bank.

Virginia, North Carolina, and Alabama joined South Carolina in denouncing the Tariff of Abominations while Massachusetts, Ohio, Pennsylvania, Rhode Island, Indiana, and New York responded with opposing resolutions in support of it. Under the new law some items, such as woolen blankets manufactured in New England and in Europe, had tariff rates of 200 percent.

Under the leadership of John C. Calhoun, South Carolina nullified the 1828 Tariff of Abominations, following a course of action pursued by other states' rights advocates, including Jefferson, when fighting unconstitutional federal usurpations of power. On November 19, 1832, a political convention was convened that adopted an ordinance of nullification, declaring the tariff act was "unauthorized by the Constitution of the United States, and violate[d] the true meaning and intent thereof." It was therefore "null, void, no law, nor binding upon this State, its officers, or citizens." As of February 1, 1833, all enforcement of tariff collection in South Carolina was to be suspended.

South Carolina meant business. The nullification law authorized importers to recover any goods that had been impounded by federal tariff collectors; sheriffs were instructed to seize the personal property of the tariff collectors and award it to the importers until their seized goods were returned; all duties were to be reimbursed to the importers with interest; tariff collectors were subject to fines and imprisonment for any attempts to resist the nullification law; and no jail in the state could be used to imprison anyone for failure to pay the tariff. A fund of $200,000 was made available to the governor of the state to purchase firearms, if necessary, to enforce the nullification law through the state militia.

President Andrew Jackson had made some threats to enforce the tariff collection, but, after further tariff increases in

1832, a lower, compromise tariff rate was finally agreed upon in 1833, and secession and war were avoided. As has been the case throughout world history, freer trade led to prosperity while protectionism threatened war. The average tariff rate would slowly be reduced over the next several decades. On the eve of the War between the States, it was at the lowest level it would ever be during the nineteenth century (about 15 percent).

## HOW TARIFFS PLUNDERED AMERICAN FARMERS

To understand why the South was so agitated over protectionist tariffs it is essential to understand how tariffs affect the economics of agriculture. Protectionist tariffs always impose a disproportionate and unjust burden on export-dependent regions within a country, and in the nineteenth century the agrarian South exported as much as three-fourths of everything it produced, especially cotton, tobacco, and rice. Exporters who sold their goods in foreign markets, mostly in Europe, found competition was so intense that they were unable to pass on *any* of their higher costs of living, caused by the tariff increases, to their customers. Northern consumers were also plundered by protectionist tariffs that drove up the prices of the manufactured goods, but since they were not predominantly exporters they had an easier time passing on the cost to *their* customers, or arguing for wage increases to maintain their standard of living. As explained in a popular international economics textbook by

> Farmers are always disproportionately harmed by high tariff rates because reduced imports impoverishes our trading partners, causing them to purchase fewer of *our* exports, especially agricultural exports.

Wilson Brown and Jan Hogendorn, which, like almost all text-books, reflects the professional consensus on various issues: "The only group that is powerless to pass the costs [of protectionist tariffs] on further are the exporters, who have to sell at world prices and swallow these costs. In essence, a tax on imports becomes a tax on exports as well."[4] So, even though the U.S. Constitution prohibits taxes on exports, taxes on imports (tariffs) have essentially the same effect: They disproportionately punish exporters through indirect means. This burden has always disproportionately harmed American farmers from all regions of the country.

Nineteenth-century Southerners understood this concept perfectly well, for they saw their incomes decline whenever tariff rates rose. In a September 1, 1828, letter to Micah Sterling of Watertown, New York, John C. Calhoun explained that "a protectionist tariff gives to one section [the North] the power of recharging . . . the duty, while to the other [the South] it is a pure unmitigated burden." This was true, wrote Calhoun, because the South "was engaged in cultivating the great staples of the country for a foreign market, in a market where we can receive no protection, and where we cannot receive one cent more to indemnify us for the heavy duties we have to pay as consumers."[5]

Calhoun knew firsthand how protectionist tariffs disproportionately harmed American exporters. In one speech before Congress he noted that "during the eight years of high duties [1824–1832], the increase of our foreign commerce . . . was almost entirely arrested; and . . . the exports of domestic manufactures actually fell off."[6] He considered protectionism to be a form of political "warfare." "Protection against what?" he rhetorically asked, and then stated the obvious answer: "Against low prices."

Nobel laureate economist Milton Friedman and his wife, Rose, explain in their bestselling book, *Free to Choose,* just why exports decline after tariffs are increased: "If tariffs are imposed on say, textiles, that will add to output and employment in the textile industry. However, foreign producers who no longer can sell their textiles in the United States earn fewer dollars. They will have less to spend in the United States. Exports will go down to balance the decreased imports."[7] In other words, mid-nineteenth-century tariffs might have benefited New England textile mill owners, but at the expense of consumers in general, and especially export-reliant farmers.

When protectionist tariffs cause a reduction in imports (which is their sole purpose), our foreign trading partners will then have fewer dollars with which to buy *our* exported goods to *their* countries—especially agricultural products. Restricting imports today will invariably cause a reduction of our own exports tomorrow. And remember, the mid-nineteenth-century South had an overwhelmingly export-oriented economy.

It wasn't just the antebellum South that complained about discriminatory tariff policy. All agricultural regions exported a large percentage of their produce in the nineteenth century and were similarly victimized by the Whig/Republican policies of protectionism. During the latter part of the century midwestern farmers became ardent free traders precisely because of tarriffs' effects on their exports. As explained by Frank Chodorov in his book *The Income Tax:* "The plight of these [midwestern] farmers was made worse by the protective tariff policy of the government. The best they could get for their products was the

> The South exported as much as three-fourths of what it produced and was economically devastated by high protectionist tariffs.

competitive world price, while manufactures they bought, from the East, were loaded down with duties. . . . The populists clamored for lower tariffs."[8] This also likely explains why so much of the Northern opposition to the Lincoln administration during the war came from the Midwest.[9]

It is also telling that in Confederate president Jefferson Davis's first inaugural address, delivered on February 18, 1861, he did not mention the word *slavery* but emphasized the fact that the South, an "agricultural people," relied crucially on free trade. "An agricultural people, whose chief interest is the export of a commodity required in every manufacturing country, our true policy is peace and the freest trade which our necessities will permit. It is alike our interest, and that of all those to whom we would sell and from whom we would buy, that there should be fewest practicable restrictions upon the interchange of commodities."[10]

## LINCOLN'S TARIFF WAR

As soon as the new Republican Party gained enough power, it succeeded in getting the U.S. House of Representatives to pass the highly protectionist Morrill Tariff during the 1859–1860 session of Congress. According to the *Congressional Globe* (precursor of the *Congressional Record*), there was only one yes vote from a secessionist state (Tennessee) and forty no votes. There were only fifteen no votes (out of 64) from Northern states.

The Republican Party used the severe recession in 1857 as an excuse to propose protectionism as a "cure." This makes no economic sense—raising prices and reducing trade to alleviate the effects of recession, unemployment, and rising poverty—but a gullible and largely economically illiterate Northern public apparently fell for it.

Protectionism was so important to the Republican Party of 1860 (and beyond) that in his book *Yankee Leviathan,* historian Richard Bensel labeled it the "keystone" of the Republican Party platform of 1860. After being elected president, Abraham Lincoln literally owed *everything,* politically, to his Northern protectionist supporters. And as a master politician he understood that he *had* to come through for them if his political career was to be a success. It was northern protectionists, especially ones from Pennsylvania and New Jersey, who catapulted him into the position of Republican Party nominee and, ultimately, the presidency. An important part of this story was told in a July 1944 article in the prestigious *American Historical Review* by Professor Reinhard H. Luthin entitled "Abraham Lincoln and the Tariff." The following discussion is based on Professor Luthin's well-documented accounts.

> Beginning in the 1820s there was almost no support for protectionist tariffs from Southern members of Congress.

Lincoln had been an ardent protectionist for his entire political career. He claimed to have made more speeches on that topic than on any other, and he stumped for the Whig Party's protectionist presidential candidates in numerous elections. In 1860 some of the most powerful and influential men in Illinois recognized that Pennsylvania, with the second-largest number of electoral votes, could be the key to winning the nomination and the presidency. They also understood that, as the heart of the iron and steel industry, the state's Republicans would demand a candidate with solid protectionist credentials. Abraham Lincoln fit the bill.

Joseph Medill, the influential editor of the *Chicago Press and Tribune,* recognized immediately that favorite son Abraham

Lincoln was the perfect candidate: In addition to his solid protectionist credentials, he was a slick politician, a trial lawyer, and a bona fide member of the Northern, moneyed, corporate elite. He editorialized in his newspaper that Lincoln was "an old Clay Whig, is right on the tariff and he is exactly right on all other issues. Is there any man who could suit Pennsylvania better?"

> Lincoln cleverly used his lifelong reputation as a staunch protectionist to secure the Republican Party nomination.

At around the same time a relative of Lincoln's by marriage, Edward Wallace of Pennsylvania, solicited Lincoln's views on the tariff by communicating through his brother, William Wallace. On October 11, 1859, Lincoln wrote Wallace the following: "My dear Sir: your brother, Dr. William Wallace, showed me a letter of yours, in which you kindly mention my name, inquire for my tariff view, and suggest the propriety of my writing a letter upon the subject. I was an old Henry Clay-Tariff Whig. In old times I made more speeches on that subject than any other. I have not changed my views."

As a masterful politician—certainly among the slickest in all of American history—Lincoln understood that if he made his protectionist views too public he would risk losing the support of agricultural regions of the country. Consequently, he asked Dr. Wallace and others he wrote to on the subject to keep their correspondence on the tariff issue confidential and private. Going a step further, he sent a personal envoy, his friend David Davis, to Pennsylvania with original copies of eleven of his pro-tariff speeches. Another personal envoy, one William Reynolds, was sent to solidify his protectionist views with the powerful Pennsylvania congressman Thaddeus Stevens.

Davis met with Republican Party leaders throughout the state in August of 1860 to show them Lincoln's speeches promoting protectionism. Pennsylvania senator Simon Cameron understood Lincoln's political dilemma and instructed Davis: "Nothing about these [speeches] must get into the newspapers," presumably so that voters in agricultural states would not learn of Lincoln's dogmatically protectionist views.[11]

Lincoln's strategy succeeded, and when the protectionist tariff plan was finally voted on at the Chicago convention, writes Luthin, "The Pennsylvania and New Jersey delegations were terrific in their applause over the tariff resolution, and their hilarity was contagious, finally pervading the whole vast auditorium."[12] One eyewitness recalled that upon passage of the protectionist plank, "one thousand tongues yelled, ten thousand hats, caps and handkerchiefs waving with the wildest fervor. Frantic jubilation."

Upon reading of this, Southern politicians must have been even more alarmed than they were in 1828 at the prospect of having their economy ruined by protectionist tariffs. When Lincoln returned home to Springfield after securing the nomination, writes Luthin, a Republican Party rally featured "an immense wagon" bearing a gigantic sign that read: "Protection for Home Industry!" This in fact was the slogan at the bottom of 1860 Republican campaign posters bearing pictures of Lincoln and his vice presidential candidate, Hannibal Hamlin.

After he was elected Lincoln publicly proclaimed that no issue—none—was more important than raising the average tariff rate.

Once elected, Lincoln openly stumped for senatorial passage of the Morrill Tariff. In a February 19, 1861, speech in Pittsburgh, Pennsylvania, he told his audience that no other issue—none—was more important to their congressional representatives than raising tariffs. President James Buchanan *of Pennsylvania* would sign the Morrill Tariff into law on March 2, 1861, two days before Lincoln's inauguration. Luthin reveals: "Morrill, John Sherman of Ohio, and Thaddeus Stevens of Pennsylvania steered the bill through the House; Simon Cameron of Pennsylvania and James F. Simmons of Rhode Island, a wealthy textile mill owner, guided it through the Senate."

In his first inaugural address Lincoln shockingly threw down the gauntlet of war over the tariff issue, literally threatening the invasion of any state that failed to collect the newly doubled tariff. On the issue of slavery he was 100 percent accommodating, going so far as to pledge his support for a constitutional amendment that would forever ban the federal government from interfering with Southern slavery. But on tariff collection he was uncompromising and dictatorial. "[T]here needs to be no bloodshed or violence, and there shall be none unless it is forced upon the national authority."

What was he talking about? What might ignite bloodshed and violence? Failure to collect the tariff, that's what. After making the obligatory statement that it was his obligation to "possess the property and places belonging to the Government" he further stated that it was his duty "to collect the duties and imposts; but beyond what may be necessary for these objects, there will be no invasion, no using force against or among the people anywhere." In other words, Pay Up or Die. Fail to collect the tariff, as the South Carolinians did in 1828, and there *will* be a military invasion, Lincoln announced. He would not back off when it came to tax

In his first inaugural address Lincoln promised a military invasion of any state that refused to collect the newly doubled tariff rate. He kept his promise.

collection, as President Andrew Jackson had done some three decades earlier.

Two weeks after Fort Sumter, Lincoln announced a naval blockade of the Southern ports as one of his first acts of war, doing so unconstitutionally, without involving Congress. The seceded states clearly had no intention of sending tariff revenues to Washington, D.C., so Lincoln announced that the purpose of the blockade was essentially to render to "Caesar" what is Caesar's. He named only one reason for the naval blockade: tariff collection. This is how America's thirty-seven-year tariff war was turned into a shooting war.

Economists Robert A. McGuire and T. Norman Van Cott surely understated their case in the peer-reviewed economics journal *Economic Inquiry* in 2002, when they concluded after analyzing the role of tariffs in precipitating the War between the States that "the tariff issue may in fact have been even more important in the North-South tensions that led to the Civil War than many economists and historians currently believe."[13]

# 14

## The Great Inflationist

When Abraham Lincoln first entered Illinois politics in 1832 he announced: "My politics are short and sweet, like the old woman's dance. I am in favor of a national bank, . . . in favor of the internal improvements system and a high protective tariff." The last two chapters have discussed the latter two policies—corporate welfare and protectionism. It is revealing that Lincoln, ever the careful wordsmith and trial lawyer, listed a national bank as his first priority.

Eighteen hundred thirty-two was the year of the big political showdown over the rechartering of the Bank of the United States (BUS). The battle pitted President Andrew Jackson against the bank's president, Nicolas Biddle. On Biddle's side was Henry Clay and what was soon to become the Whig Party establishment, including Lincoln. In opposition stood the descendants of the Jeffersonian political tradition, which was especially strong in the South.

A national bank was arguably the lifeblood of the Whig Party, and the main reason for its coming into existence in the early 1830s. Few politicians of the era were more devoted to resurrecting the bank than Abraham Lincoln was. In *The Rise and Fall of the American Whig Party,* University of Virginia historian Michael Holt wrote of how, during the 1840, 1844, and 1848 national elections Lincoln "crisscrossed the state [of Illinois] ardently and eloquently defending specific Whig programs like a national bank." Not only did he defend the programs, writes Holt, but "few people in the party were so committed to its economic agenda as Lincoln."[1]

University of Georgia economist Richard Timberlake, author of a treatise on American monetary history entitled *Monetary Policy of the United States,* agreed with Professor Holt's assessment of the importance of central banking to the Whigs. "To the Whigs . . . a national bank was their life—the vital principle—without which they could not live as a party—the power which was to give them power. . . . To lose it, was to lose the fruits of the election, with the prospect of losing the party itself."[2]

> The first reason Lincoln gave for entering politics in 1832 was that he wanted to crusade for a nationalized banking system.

In other words, the Whigs always intended to use a national bank, and its printing of paper money that was not redeemable in gold or silver, as the means of financing the colossal patronage schemes that they hoped would keep them in power indefinitely.

## THE GREAT BANK WAR

The best published account of the conflict between Andrew Jackson and Nicolas Biddle over the BUS is Robert Remini's *Andrew Jackson and the Bank War.* Remini explains how Jackson considered paper money that was not redeemable in gold or silver to be "the instrument of the swindler and the cheat." For Jackson "hard money—specie [i.e., gold or silver] was the only legitimate money; anything else was a fraud to steal from honest men."[3]

Jackson also believed that, in light of the importance of states' rights in protecting liberty, a national bank was unconstitutional. The Supreme Court eventually disagreed with him. Richard Timberlake explains why this belief—that a national bank posed the threat of a dangerous centralization of political power—was so pervasive at the time: "The states . . . were properly jealous and fearful of encroachment by the federal government. Since a central bank would necessarily be a federal bank and would maintain and operate state branches from a distant center, proponents of states' rights found opposition to a national bank almost mandatory."[4]

Jackson feared that a central bank would be controlled by Northern bankers and would be used to manipulate politics, to the detriment of the economy and the public. Remini points out that the strongest support for the bank came from New England, whereas the fiercest opposition originated in the South.

Jackson had good reason to fear a politically manipulated central bank. The first president of the BUS was a U.S. Navy captain named William Jones, who had no banking experience and who had just gone personally bankrupt. He was politically well connected, however, and was awarded the job despite his complete lack of credentials. In *The Panic of 1819*, economist Murray Rothbard blamed Jones for creating the "panic," America's first serious depression.[5]

The bank's second president was Nicolas Biddle, who continued to politicize it. Remini documents how Biddle granted below-market interest rate loans and "consulting contracts" to members of Congress who promised to support the bank. These loans and "consulting fees" were essentially political kickbacks paid with taxpayers' dollars deposited in the BUS. Jackson's treasury secretary Roger B. Taney, the future chief justice of the United States, complained of the bank's "corrupting influence" and its "patronage greater than that of the government." What he probably had in mind was the sort of shenanigans documented by Henry Clay biographer Maurice Baxter in his book *Henry Clay and the American System*. Clay left Congress for three years beginning in 1822 after having incurred some $40,000 in personal debt to become the general counsel of the BUS. His income from the bank "apparently amounted to what he needed to pay off his personal debts," wrote Baxter. "When he resigned to become secretary of state in 1825, he was pleased with his compensation."[6]

Another prominent Whig, Daniel Webster, did not even bother to resign from Congress before collecting bribes and kickbacks from the BUS. Baxter writes of how Webster simply demanded a "retainer" from Biddle, "If it be wished that my relation to the Bank should be continued."[7]

Biddle further proved Andrew Jackson's charges of political corruption and ma-

Jefferson—and the Jeffersonians—fiercely opposed a nationalized bank, which they thought would be corrupting and economically destabilizing. They were right; Lincoln and the Whigs were wrong.

nipulation to be true when, during the 1828 national election campaign, he spent more than $100,000 of the bank's deposits in support of Jackson's political opponents; promised BUS money to friendly politicians to spend on "internal improvements" in their districts and states in return for their votes; paid for the printing of Henry Clay's speeches in support of the BUS;

and paid for newspaper ads that promoted himself and the bank and attacked Jackson.

When the U.S. Supreme Court issued an opinion that the BUS was constitutional, Jackson essentially said "thank you for your opinion, but my opinion is different—and equally valid." At that time the Court was not yet the final arbiter of constitutionality, as it has been since 1865. In response to Justice Marshall's opinion on the bank, Jackson said this:

> To this conclusion I cannot assent. Congress and the president as well as the Court must each for itself be guided by its own opinion of the Constitution . . . the opinion of the judges has no more authority over Congress than the opinion of Congress has over the judges, and on that point the president is independent of both. The authority of the Supreme Court must not, therefore, be permitted to control the Congress or the executive when acting in their legislative capacities.[8]

Jackson proceeded to defund the Bank.

The rhetorical battle over a central bank would continue on for the next several decades, with the likes of Clay, Webster, and Lincoln advocating a reinstitution of the bank on the one hand, and such Jeffersonians as Calhoun and President John Tyler on the other, in opposition.

## LINCOLN'S ROLE IN AMERICA'S THIRTY-YEAR BANK WAR

The demise of the BUS led to the creation of a new banking system known as the Independent Treasury System. It was established in 1840, ended in 1841 by the Whigs, who had temporarily gained power, and then reestablished in 1846. It would be the prevailing banking system of the United States until Lincoln's administration ended it in 1862. The reign of the Independent Treasury System was known as the "free-banking era."

One of the major issues of contention during the great banking debate was whether or not currency should be redeemable in gold or silver. The Jeffersonians said yes, it should be, as a means of limiting the ability of banks to create inflation and to artificially boost the economy from time to time, creating boom-and-bust cycles in the economy. Money that was not redeemable in specie, asserted the Jeffersonians, was essentially counterfeit and would invariably lead to economic hardship.

The Whigs, and later the Republicans, were obsessed with solidifying their political power through patronage financed precisely by the printing of paper money that was *not* redeemable in gold or silver. They made nonsensical arguments that inflationary finance was somehow good for the nation's economy, but such arguments were vacuous even to economists at the time.

Under the Independent Treasury System the only legally recognizable money was gold and silver coins; all currency was redeemable on demand in those two precious metals. Banks were largely incapable of inflating their currencies under this system, to the chagrin of the Whigs. If they did, and did not have enough gold and silver on hand, then they simply went bankrupt. That's why such prominent economic historians as Jeffrey Hummel and Richard Timberlake have praised the system in their writings. Hummel has studied the free-banking era and has concluded that, though it had its flaws, it was the most stable banking system the U.S. has ever had.[9] Timberlake concluded that the Independent Treasury System was perhaps the "optimal" monetary system within the framework of the gold standard, which the country was on at the time.

Like his political role model and party leader, Henry Clay, Lincoln was fiercely opposed to the Independent Treasury System, for it robbed the Whigs of the opportunity to finance their corporate welfare giveaways with paper money not backed by gold or silver. On December 26, 1839, he gave a speech in opposition to the system and in support of inflationary finance through the mechanism of what economists call "fiat money." The long-winded speech was a fiery denunciation of the responsible policies of the Independent Treasury System, condemning it as guilty of generating economic instability, being administratively costly compared to other systems, an insecure depository of money, and prone to reducing the quantity of money in circulation. None of these charges turned out to be true.

> Like other Northern Whigs, Lincoln was strongly opposed to sound money redeemable in gold.

Much of Lincoln's speech was simply absurd. He claimed, for example, that requiring banks to hold reserves of gold or silver would lead to a situation where "all [will] suffer more or less, and very many will lose everything that renders life desirable." Thus, to Lincoln the Independent Treasury was such a bad idea that it may well lead to a national suicide epidemic! Such is bound to be the case with many who lose "everything that renders life desirable."

Lincoln was not a religious man, never joined a church, and never admitted to having become a Christian, but he was masterful at invoking religious rhetoric in his political speeches to audiences of believers. In this speech he said: "The Savior of the world chose twelve disciples, and even one of that small number, selected by superhuman wisdom, turned out a traitor and a devil. And, it may not be improper here to add, that Judas carried the bag—was the Sub-Treasurer of the Savior and his disciples."

The point here is that the Independent Treasury System, and its "Sub-Treasurer" was supposedly traitorous to the American public, just as Judas betrayed Jesus Christ. Just as eliminating Judas may have saved Jesus from persecution, Lincoln insinuated, so could America be "saved" (and all those suicides averted) by eliminating the Independent Treasury System and allowing a Whig government to print paper money like mad in order to finance its agenda of corporate welfare for canal- and railroad-building corporations.

About a year later Lincoln was in a leadership position in the Illinois legislature and repeatedly opposed proposals by the Democrats in the legislature to audit the Illinois State Bank. The bank had been bankrolling many unsuccessful and never-completed "internal improvement" boondoggles that Lincoln and the Illinois Whigs were responsible for. The last thing they wanted was an audit of the books.

Then, in December of 1840, the Illinois Democrats wanted to require the bank to make payments in gold and silver instead of paper money. Lincoln wanted desperately to avoid this outcome, so on the day the vote was to be taken to require specie redemption he bolted for the door and instructed his fellow Whigs to follow him. Without a quorum the legislature could not vote to adjourn, and the suspension of specie payment would continue a while longer.[10] Lincoln quickly discovered the door had been locked and guarded at the instruction of the Democratic Party leadership, so he literally jumped out of the first-floor window, followed by his lemming-like Whig compatriots.

Thereafter the Democrats in the legislature called him "Leaping Lincoln and his flying brethren." The stunt failed; Illinois adopted honest money; and Lincoln and the Whigs were defeated once again.

In his book *What Has Government Done to Our Money,* economist Murray Rothbard clearly explained the significance of the phrase "suspension of specie payment" that was the source of all the conflict and controversy. This explanation clarifies just what it was that Abraham Lincoln and his fellow Whigs and Republicans were so doggedly determined to achieve for so many decades:

> The bluntest way for government to foster . . . inflation is to grant banks the special privilege of refusing to pay their obligations, while yet continuing in their operation. While everyone else must pay their debts or go bankrupt, the banks are permitted to refuse redemption of their receipts, at the same time forcing their own debtors to pay when their loans fall due. The usual name for this is "a suspension of specie payments." A more accurate name would be "license for theft," for what else can we call a government permission to continue business without fulfilling one's contract?[11]

With the success of the Independent Treasury System the Whigs were unable to deliver on their many promises of patronage. This is why Professor Timberlake remarked that, to Whigs like Lincoln, a national bank was nothing less than their reason for existing as a political party. They failed to "deliver" protectionist tariffs as well during the 1833–1853 period, and the party imploded. Constituencies who favored protectionism, corporate welfare, and national banking became Republicans.

When Lincoln became president, and the Southern Democrats had left the Congress, the old Whig coalition was finally entrenched in power. It immediately raised tariff rates ten times, commenced the building of a government-subsidized transcontinental railroad, and replaced the Independent Treasury System with a nationalized money supply. On February 25, 1862, the Legal Tender Act empowered the secretary of the Treasury to issue paper money ("greenbacks") that was not immediately redeemable in gold or silver. The National Currency Acts of 1863 and 1864 created a system of nationally chartered banks that could issue bank notes supplied to them by the new comptroller of the currency, and placed a 10 percent tax on state bank notes (currency issued by private banks chartered by state governments) to drive them out of business and establish a federal monetary monopoly for the first time in American history. Although the printing of paper money that was not redeemable in specie amounted to legalized counterfeiting, the Secret Service was also created to police private counterfeiting. If there was to be counterfeiting, the U.S. government was to have a monopoly in it.

> It was the Lincoln administration that finally nationalized the nation's money supply, after a seventy-year political battle.

This ended once and for all the separation of money and state in America. As economist Murray Rothbard wrote in his treatise *A History of Money and Banking in the United States,* "In that way, the Republican Party, which inherited the Whig admiration for paper money and governmental control and sponsorship of inflationary banking, was able to implant the soft-money tradition permanently in the American system."[12] As the government's paper money flooded the banks, "greenback" dollars became so devalued that by July 1864 they were worth only 35 cents in gold, even though they were not issued until mid-1863.

A nationalized money supply helped transform America from a constitutional republic to an empire.

The Republican Party establishment created a system whereby almost all currency was issued by just a few Wall Street banks closely affiliated with the party. In *The Greatest Nation on the Earth* historian Heather Cox Richardson quotes Senator John Sherman as saying that the party's objective was "to nationalize as much as possible, even the currency, so as to make men love their country before their states. All private interests, all local interests, all banking interests, the interests of individuals, everything, should be subordinate now to the interest of the Government." This statement could not possibly be any further away from Jefferson's "that government governs best which governs least" philosophy. The Republicans, including Lincoln, clearly saw the nationalization of the money supply as an essential weapon in their crusade to abolish Jeffersonianism, centralize governmental power in Washington, D.C., and finally implement the Hamiltonian system of protectionism, national debt, nationalized banking, and corporate welfare.

The sponsor of the banking legislation in the U.S. House of Representatives was Congressman Elbridge G. Spaulding, a banker from Buffalo, New York. Spaulding rejoiced that the new monetary system would finally clear the way for unlimited patronage spending by his party, something that politicians like himself (and Lincoln) had been crusading for for many years.

Richardson quotes a *New York Times* editorial on March 9, 1863, that celebrated this long-sought political victory. "The legal tender act and the national currency bill crystallized . . . a centralization of power, such as Hamilton might have eulogized as magnificent."[13]

Kentucky Democrat Lazarus Powell was not as enthusiastic, writes Richardson. "The result of this legislation is to utterly destroy the rights of the states. It is asserting a power which if carried out to its logical result would enable the national Congress to destroy every institution of the States and cause all power to be concentrated here [in Washington, D.C.]."[14] Lincoln, Sherman, Stevens, and other Republican Party luminaries must have been smiling and nodding their heads in approval upon hearing this remark.

The Party of Lincoln set out to fundamentally transform the American government from a decentralized confederacy of sovereign states to a consolidated, monolithic *empire* that could interfere with the affairs of other nations. They succeeded, and the nationalization of the money supply was always considered to be an indispensable component of their success. As Richardson further explains: "By 1863 the Republicans envisioned a dominant *international* role for a unified American nation, and Sherman promised that the bank bill, with its implicit strengthening of the national government, would advance that goal."[15] These Republicans were "building a new economic role for an increasingly powerful national government, permanently involving it in the country's monetary affairs." That's why Abraham Lincoln deserves the designation of "the great inflationist" along with all of his other titles.

# PART III

# The Politics of the Lincoln Cult

# 15

## Making Cannon Fodder

I n his book *Making Patriots,* Walter Berns of the American
Enterprise Institute in Washington, D.C., argues that the tra-
ditional American philosophy of individualism, with its dictum
that the role of government is to secure inalienable rights to life,
liberty, and the pursuit of happiness for all citizens, creates a serious dilemma for the American state. The dilemma is that
young people who are primarily concerned with pursuing their
own education and careers, and raising their families, will not be
sufficiently motivated to join the military and risk their lives for
"abstract ideas" that, says Berns, are bigger and more important
than the individual lives of America's youth.

"We cannot be indifferent to the welfare of others," writes
Berns, no matter where in the world those others may reside.
Consequently, America's youth must be prepared, or so he says,
to sacrifice their lives not in defense of their own country but
"for the welfare of others" all over the globe. Editorialists like
Berns apparently think of themselves as more or less philosopher kings who will decide which parts of the globe are in need
of "salvation" at the hands of the U.S. military. They want to

send the nation's youth to fight and die for these abstract causes (like "democracy in the Middle East"), while *they* remain safe and sound in their academic or think tank offices.

The dilemma, says Berns, is how to motivate America's youth to become such sacrificial lambs for the state. The answer is to devise a new "civil religion" so that young people will think of themselves as "religious" crusaders as they march off to war. Not genuine religion, but a religion that worships the state and its dictates, as defined by gatekeeping intellectuals like Berns.

In short, Berns calls for nothing less than a complete repudi-ation of the American ideal, as expressed in the Declaration of Independence, that citizens have inalienable rights to life, lib-erty, and the pursuit of happiness, *and* that the purpose of gov-ernment is to secure these rights, period. Under this philosophy the citizens are the masters of their government, which only ex-ists to serve them by securing their rights. Under Berns's philos-ophy it's the other way around: the people, particularly young people, are to *serve—and even die for—the state* to promote the state's whims and abstract notions, such as the forceful imposi-tion of "democracy" around the world. Under this scenario, the state is the master and the people are its servants. Patriotism re-ally is the last refuge of the scoundrel.

> The Lincoln cult believes the Lincoln legend should be used to convince America's youth that it's not so bad after all to become cannon fodder.

To inspire "patriotism" in the nation's youth, a "national poet" must mesmerize them and unite them in a cause, says Berns. Ideally, such a poet can convince them to aban-don their individualism, their old-fashioned Americanism, and their selfish pursuit of peace-ful and prosperous lives. Fortunately, Berns informs us, such a national poet is at hand. That person is Abraham Lincoln, whom he describes as "statesman, poet, and . . . the martyred Christ of democracy's passion play."[1] If America's youth are to be persuaded to become the American equivalent of mad Muslim fanatics hell-bent on a "civil" religious revolution, then they must be indoctrinated in Lincoln's "greatness," which consists not so much in his actions but "in the power and beauty of his words."[2]

This is typical behavior of a member of the Lincoln cult: they concentrate almost exclusively on a small sampling of Lincoln's nicer-sounding political speeches, while often showing little or no interest in his actual *behavior* or real history. This is a disastrous recipe for understanding *any* politician. Any politician who has ever served in a national office can be made to appear as a "great statesman" or a "great humanitarian" if he is judged exclusively by his own political rhetoric.

Another typical characteristic of Lincoln cultists is to ascribe angelic motives to everything Lincoln ever said or did, and pretending to possess unique knowledge of what was "in his heart," if not his mind. This theme runs throughout the voluminous Lincoln literature, including *Making Patriots,* in which Berns devotes more than a chapter to fabricating myths about Lincoln that he apparently hopes will become part of the "civil religion" of American militarism and imperialism.

Many of the statements made by Berns are so absurd that they can only be construed as pure nonsense. For example, he writes that Lincoln responded to Fort Sumter, where no one was even wounded let alone killed, with a full-scale invasion of all the Southern states, including a naval blockade, because "his purpose was peace."[3] Thus, in a statement that defines the word *Orwellian,* Berns literally says that war is peace. Berns believes Lincoln ordered his army to kill fellow citizens by the hundreds of thousands in the name of peace. Before the war broke out, both Confederate peace commissioners and Napoleon III of France attempted to broker a peace, but Lincoln refused to even meet with them to discuss it. Lincoln rebuffed every opportunity to discuss peace, yet to Berns "his purpose was peace," not war.

> Lincoln cultist Walter Berns believes that Lincoln waged war on Southern *civilians* for four long years because he loved them and was "a man of peace."

Lincoln illegally suspended the writ of habeas corpus and had his military imprison tens of thousands of Northern political critics and opponents without due process; he censored all telegraph communication; shut down over three hundred opposition newspapers; imprisoned dozens of duly elected officials of the state of Maryland; participated in the rigging of Northern elections; waged war without the consent of Congress; illegally created a new state, West Virginia; and deported the most outspoken member of the Democratic opposition, Congressman Clement L. Vallandigham of Ohio. Generations of historians have admitted that no one considered any of this to have been legal or constitutional. But to Berns, all of this was done "so that the laws be faithfully executed." This is the same absurd argument that Lincoln himself asserted, and it is no less absurd when coming from a "distinguished fellow" of the American Enterprise Institute 140 years later. Lincoln's massive disregard for the law and the Constitution, according to Berns, is evidence of his devotion to the law and the Constitution.

Lincoln never became a Christian and was opposed by nearly every minister in Springfield, Illinois, when he first ran for president. Yet to Berns, Lincoln "of course . . . read the Bible" and used biblical language "to save the American Republic . . . with his words."[4]

The *voluntary* union of the founding fathers was not "saved" but destroyed. It was no longer voluntary after the war. Moreover, it wasn't so much Lincoln's political *rhetoric* that achieved this result as it was the work of the largest and best equipped army in the history of the world up to that point. An army that, on Lincoln's orders as commander in chief, waged war on civilians as well as on military combatants for four long years. Lincoln's armies bombed Southern cities, killing thousands of civilians. Homes, farms, and businesses were pillaged, plundered, and burned all throughout the South. He compulsively experimented with bigger and bigger weapons of mass destruction to be turned loose on Southern civilians as well as on the Confederate army. But to Berns, "Lincoln never looked upon the Confederates as enemies."[5]

He micromanaged a war that killed his fellow citizens by the hundreds of thousands and maimed more than double that amount because he loved them, claims Walter Berns, and he supposedly "purged his heart and mind from hatred or even anger towards his fellow-countrymen of the South."[6] There's that technique again that is so typical of Lincoln cultists—claiming to know what was in the heart and mind of a man who died over a century ago. Obviously, one must possess psychic powers in order to become a certified "Lincoln scholar."

Lincoln famously said of General Ulysses S. Grant that he admired him and would stick with him as the commander of the Army of the Potomac because "he fights." In other words, Grant was a general who would never stop killing his fellow citizens, no matter how many of his own men were sacrificed in the process. To Berns, behavior like this is apparently proof that Lincoln "loved" Southerners.

Berns asserts that a war resulting in the death of some 620,000 Americans, including one out of four Southern men of military age, taught Americans "to love the Union" and "helped make us patriots." But surely Americans from the Southern states were not taught by the war "to love the Union." Millions of Southerners hated and despised the newly consolidated government, run for decades after the war by the Republican Party as a one-party monopoly. What Berns means by "loving the Union" is submitting blind obedience to the dictates of the state. He conflates the word *country* with *government,* something the founding fathers would never have done.

The "greatest importance" of the Lincoln legend, says Berns, is that it has been used for generations "in the public schools" where "we" were taught "to love our country."

> The Lincoln legend has helped teach our children blind obedience to the American state, a quintessentially un-American practice.

The deification of Lincoln after the war went a long way toward deifying the presidency itself, and the American state. This is what Berns approves of so fervently: a practice that would likely motivate many of the founders to reach for their swords and muskets and fight another revolution.

*Making Patriots* by Walter Berns is an example of how the Lincoln legend is full of myths, misinformation, and distortions of history. The purpose of the myths and distortions is to attach the "moral authority" of Lincoln to various political agendas, which, in Berns's case, is foreign policy imperialism.

# 16

## Lincolnite Totalitarians

I n his book *Patriotic Gore: Studies in the Literature of the Civil War,* literary critic Edmund Wilson explained that one of the most important consequences of the war was the establishment of a strong central government. In this regard, he considered Lincoln to be connected politically to Lenin and Bismarck, who, like Lincoln, were the figures primarily responsible for introducing large, centralized, governmental bureaucracy into their own respective countries.[1]

Each of these men, wrote Wilson, "became an uncompromising dictator" and was succeeded by newly formed bureaucracies that continued to expand the power of the state and diminish freedom so that "all the bad potentialities of the policies he had initiated were realized, after his removal, in the most undesirable ways."

The Lincoln cult has succeeded in sweeping almost all such statements under the rug for generations, so that most Americans—even most Southerners—have never even had a negative thought about Lincoln. But it was not always that way. The Lincoln cult was not always so influential. Until around the mid-1960s it was still possible to find objective scholarship, as opposed to myth, fantasy, and idolatry, in the literature on Lincoln and his war. One example is an August 24, 1965, article in the "conservative" *National Review* magazine by the publication's editor, Frank Meyer. Commenting on the book *Freedom Under Lincoln* by Dean Sprague, Meyer wrote that Lincoln's "pivotal role in our history was essentially negative to the genius of freedom of our country." This was so because of, among other things, the "harshness of his repressive policies and his responsibility for methods of waging war approaching the horror of total war."[2]

"Under the spurious slogan of Union," wrote Meyer, Lincoln "moved at every point . . . to consolidate central power and render nugatory the autonomy of the states. . . . It is on his shoulders that the responsibility for the war must be placed." And, "We all know his gentle words, 'with malice toward none, with charity toward all,'. . . but his actions belie this rhetoric." Here Meyer was referring to Lincoln's "repressive dictatorship" in the Northern states during the war, and the "brigand campaigns waged against civilians by Sherman," among other things.[3]

Meyer was well aware that Lincoln did not invade the South to free the slaves but to "consolidate" political power in Washington, D.C., by destroying the secession movement, as Lincoln himself had proclaimed. He also understood that all other countries of the world that ended slavery in the nineteenth century did so peacefully through compensated emancipation.

Moreover, there were very negative, long-term consequences of Lincoln's actions, just as Edmund Wilson surmised. In Meyer's mind, "Were it not for the wounds that Lincoln inflicted upon the Constitution, it would have been infinitely more difficult for Franklin Roosevelt to carry through his revolution [and] for the coercive welfare state to come into being. . . . Lincoln, I would maintain, undermined the constitutional safeguards of freedom as he opened the way to centralized government with all its attendant political evils."[4]

One no longer reads any objective articles on this subject in "establishment" conservative publications such as *National Review, The Weekly Standard,* or the publications of the American Enterprise Institute, Heritage Foundation, and especially the Claremont Institute. Quite the contrary: On the topic of Lincoln there is only room for idolatry of the sort espoused by Walter Berns and Harry Jaffa.

After Meyer's article appeared, the magazine's publisher, William F. Buckley, Jr., took him to task over it and disputed his own editor's comments on Lincoln. From that point on, there was very little realistic analysis of the Lincoln legacy in *National Review* or in most other conservative publications. An intellectual purge, of sorts, had taken place, part of an overall purge of the Old Right writers and their ideas.

Buckley successfully re-created the conservative movement in the 1950s by using his role as publisher of *National Review* to flush out many of the old, limited-government constitutionalists from the movement. In their place, Buckley promoted big government conservatives, known today as "neoconservatives." It turns out, however, that there's nothing "neo" about them: They've *always* been opposed to limited government, the defining characteristic of genuine old-fashioned conservativism.

Murray Rothbard expressed this in a January 25, 1952, article in *The Commonweal* magazine.[5] He quoted Buckley, in his (Buckley's) own words, as favoring "the extensive and productive tax laws that are needed to support a vigorous anti-communist foreign policy . . . we have got to accept Big Government for the duration [of the cold war]—for neither an offensive nor a defensive war can be waged . . . except through the instrumentality of *a totalitarian bureaucracy within our shores* (emphasis added)."[6]

We must all support, said Buckley, "large armies and air forces, atomic energy, central intelligence, war production boards [i.e., centrally planned economies], and the attendant centralization of power in Washington. . . ." The founder of *National Review* was "a totalitarian socialist," Rothbard wrote, "and what is more admits it." What other label would one give an advocate of "totalitarian bureaucracy" as his preferred form of government?

This is why Buckley personally repudiated Frank Meyer's views on Lincoln, and why most conservatives have been Lincoln idolaters ever since. Lincoln's dictatorial methods, and his creation of a consolidated, militaristic state, have long been the model for the American Right. When the cold war ended and there was no longer any need for a "totalitarian bureaucracy within our shores" the conservative movement, which now calls itself the "neoconservative" movement, declared that its new goal would be perpetual global warfare in the name of spreading democracy around the globe. Naturally, they constantly make use of the Lincoln legend in speeches and articles to attempt to "justify" this quintessentially un-American policy. They are Lincolnite totalitarians.

William F. Buckley, Jr., believed that America needed a "totalitarian bureaucracy" to fight the cold war, and that the Lincoln administration served as an ideal model.

The American state's "totalitarian bureaucracy" has grown increasingly powerful in recent years by employing such tactics as the Patriot Act, strip searches at airports, Internet spying by the government, illegally spying on millions of private phone conversations, prying into citizens' private financial records, military tribunals, torture of prisoners, and many other ominous developments that are destructive of civil liberties. And the Lincoln idolatry continues, as the name of the "martyred saint" is frequently invoked to justify such policies.

Right-wing totalitarians are not the only ones who invoke the Lincoln legend when justifying monopolistic or dictatorial government. There are many prominent academic leftists who idolize Lincoln because they, too, favor "totalitarian bureaucracy," as long as *they*, and not people like William F. Buckley, Jr., are running it. One of the best examples is Civil War historian Eric Foner of Columbia University, a past president of the American Historical Association and a self-described Marxist.

For decades, Foner was an apologist for Soviet communism. After the collapse of Soviet communism in 1989, a Moscow display of the Soviet gulag system drew a bitter denunciation by Foner, who complained of "the obsessive need to fill in the blank pages in the history of the Soviet era."[7]

Genuine conservatives were always shocked and alarmed at the totalitarian practices of the Lincoln administration.

This is indeed an odd statement for a historian to make—that it is "obsessive" to want to document the history of one of the governments that dominated global politics during the twentieth century.

In his 1988 book *The Story of American Freedom*, Foner lavishly praised the Communist Party U.S.A. as a "cultural front that helped to redraw the boundaries of American freedom." To Eric Foner communism means "freedom" and opposition to communism means tyranny. No wonder he's considered to be a top "Lincoln scholar." Foner was such an apologist for Soviet communism that he opposed the breakup of the Soviet Union and,

naturally, invoked the Lincoln legend as the reason for his opposition. In an editorial in the February 11, 1991, issue of *The
Nation* magazine entitled "Lincoln's Lesson," Foner railed against
the secession movements in Latvia, Lithuania, Estonia, and
Georgia and urged Mikhail Gorbachev to deal with them in
the same brutal manner that Lincoln dealt with the Southern
secessionists.

Marxist historians like Columbia University's Eric Foner, who opposed the breakup of the Soviet Union, naturally point to the Lincoln regime as "justification" for their position.

The entire free world was ecstatic over the collapse of Soviet communism, and no one was as thrilled as the people of the Soviet empire. But to Foner the secession of the Soviet republics was a "crisis" that would destroy the "laud-
able goal" of creating a monopolistic, dictatorial government
in the name of socialism. Such a government, Foner said,
demanded "overreaching loyalty to the Soviet Union," just as
Lincoln demanded overreaching loyalty to himself and his government. No "leader of a powerful nation," Foner complained,
should allow such a thing to happen as "the dismemberment of
the Soviet Union."[8]

He agreed completely with Edmund Wilson's characteriza-
tion of Lincoln's role in creating a consolidated, monopolistic
government, but like all totalitarian socialists, he thinks it was a
*good* thing. Socialism cannot survive if there are competing sov-
ereignties. Thus, all socialists, whether left-wing socialists like
Foner or right-wing socialists like Buckley, favor highly centralized, dictatorial government with a "strong executive."

Foner concluded his essay by opining that "The Civil War
was a central step in the consolidation of national authority in
the United States." Unlike Wilson and Frank Meyer, he viewed

this as a *positive* development. "The Union, Lincoln passionately believed, was a permanent government," Foner continued, and he hoped that "Gorbachev would surely agree."

It turns out, of course, that Gorbachev did not agree (thank God). Unlike Lincoln, the communist dictator of the Soviet Union did not have the stomach for ordering the Russian military to bomb its own cities and kill fellow citizens by the hundreds of thousands (or millions, with today's military technology) merely for the sake of "saving the [Soviet] Union."

Thus, the writings of right-wing neoconservatives as well as left-wing academics routinely invoke the mythical Lincoln legend in order to push their respective political agendas, whether it is foreign policy imperialism, as in the former case, or opining about the "unfortunate" demise of totalitarian socialism in the latter case.

Politics is a dirty business, which is why there is so often a vicious personal reaction by the likes of Eric Foner and neoconservative Lincoln idolaters to any and all writers who question some of the historical myths they have fabricated or perpetuated. They are also afraid to death of being exposed as proponents of totalitarian bureaucracy while posing as "freedom fighters" (like Foner) or strict constuctionists (like Harry Jaffa and his followers).

# 17

## Pledging Allegiance to the Omnipotent Lincolnian State

Most Americans believe that the Pledge of Allegiance to the flag was the work of the eighteenth-century founding fathers. In fact, the Pledge did not come about until 1892. It was authored by Francis Bellamy, a defrocked Baptist minister from Boston who identified himself as a "Christian Socialist" and was removed from the pulpit for preaching politics, specifically for espousing the view that "Jesus was a socialist."

Bellamy was the cousin of Edward Bellamy, author of the popular 1888 socialist fantasy *Looking Backward*. In this novel the main character, Julian West, falls asleep in 1887 and awakens in the year 2000 when "socialist utopia" had been achieved. All industry is state owned, Soviet style, and everyone is conscripted into the military at age twenty-one, is an employee of the state for their entire lives, and retires at age forty-five. All workers earn exactly the same income regardless of merit, performance, or skill. It may be hard to fathom in the twenty-first century, but there used to be many influential novelists and opinion makers who actually believed that this system—which later came to be known as totalitarian communism—would produce "utopia" or heaven on earth.

Pledge of Allegiance author Francis Bellamy said that one purpose of the Pledge was to help achieve this totalitarian fantasy in America.[1] The "true reason for allegiance to the flag," said Bellamy, was to indoctrinate schoolchildren into the Lincolnian theory of the "perpetual" nature of the consolidated, unitary, and omnipotent state. It was to ingrain in the minds of America's schoolchildren the falsehood that no such thing as state sovereignty ever existed. As discussed in the previous chapter, totalitarians of all persuasions, including Christian Socialists, have long understood that omnipotent government cannot be achieved if the citizens have divided loyalties. Federalism is poison to socialism and socialists.

Although Lincoln proved his theory to be correct—in his own mind—by force of arms, in the late nineteenth century there were still millions of Americans who cherished the Jeffersonian ideal of limited decentralized government and states' rights, and were suspicious of centralized

> The Pledge of Allegiance was authored in the late nineteenth century by a Socialist who designed it as a propaganda tool with which to brainwash children in the supposed virtues of the monopolistic, consolidated, Lincolnite state.

governmental power. Ideas cannot be snuffed out as easily as human lives or even governments can be. This was alarming to the Bellamy cousins, for they understood perfectly well that their socialist utopia could never be achieved in America unless the central government became all powerful and the notion of state sovereignty was destroyed completely. In Francis Bellamy's own words, as recounted by author John W. Baer:

The true reason for allegiance to the Flag is the "republic for which it stands." . . . And what does that vast thing, the Republic mean? It is the concise political word for the Nation—the One Nation which the Civil War was fought to prove. To make that One Nation idea clear, we must specify that it is indivisible, as Webster and Lincoln used to repeat in their great speeches.[2]

Bellamy considered the "liberty and justice for all" phrase in the Pledge of Allegiance to be an Americanized expression of the French—not the American—Revolution: "Liberty, Equality, Fraternity." The basic philosophy of the French Revolution, coming from Rousseau, was that there existed in the mind of an elite the notion or definition of "the general will," and that the elite was obligated to impose that will on the entire nation, even if it meant killing dissenters. There was to be a "single body" with "a single will," said Rousseau. Whoever disagrees with the state-sanctioned "general will" will be "forced to be free," even if it literally kills them.

In *America the Virtuous* Catholic University philosophy professor Claes Ryn explains how Rousseau's (and the Bellamy cousins') philosophy of government "collides head on with advocates of constitutionalism," such as the American founding fathers.[3] "Rousseau's wish to free the current majority from all restrictions, to dissolve the people into a homogenous mass, abolish decentralization, and remove representative institutions could not be in sharper contrast to American traditions of constitutionalism, federalism, localism, and representation."[4]

Rousseau was one of the founders of "modern nationalism," with Lincoln following in his footsteps. For Rousseau, nationalism was connected to virtue. The "general will" was said to be virtuous, by definition, and dissenters, naturally, were the opposite, sinful. It was imperative, said Rousseau, to therefore "begin by making [citizens] love their country" through indoctrination in "patriotism."[5] This is exactly what the Bellamy cousins hoped to achieve with the Pledge of Allegiance to the unitary American state, and it is also what such Lincoln cultists like Walter Berns and Harry Jaffa hope to achieve. They are truly neo-Jacobins.

Francis Bellamy claimed to have gotten the idea for the Pledge of Allegiance from the "loyalty oaths" that Southerners were forced to take, often at gunpoint, during the War between the States. The Pledge was first published in the September 1892 issue of *The Youth's Companion,* which was sort of the *Reader's Digest* of its day. At the time, Francis Bellamy had been defrocked as a minister and was the vice president in charge of education for the "Society of Christian Socialists," a national organization that advocated income taxation, central banking, nationalized education, nationalization of industry, and other features of socialism. In his book *Socialism,* economist Ludwig von Mises characterized Christian socialism as "merely a variety of socialism" and nothing exceptional. Its advocates held that "agriculture and handicraft, with perhaps small shop keeping, are the only admissible occupations. Trade and speculation are superfluous, injurious, and evil. Factories and large-scale industries are the wicked invention of the 'Jewish spirit'; they produce only bad goods which are foisted on buyers by the large stores and by other monstrosities of modern trade to the detriment of purchasers."[6]

The "one nation, indivisible" language of the Pledge was extremely important to the Bellamy cousins. If states' rights, let alone secession, were ever legitimized, then their dream of a socialist utopia in America, enforced by a unitary, dictatorial government, would never be realized. Thus, once compulsory

attendance laws were established for public schools, they provided the ideal vehicle for socialist indoctrination under the
guise of "patriotism," which in reality meant blind obedience to
the state.

The public schools were happy to assist in the cause. In 1892
the Bellamy cousins planned a "National Public School Celebra-
tion," the first major propaganda campaign to be launched on
behalf of the Pledge of Allegiance. It was a massive, nationwide
campaign that involved government schools and politicians
throughout the country. Government-run schools, along with
the Pledge, were promoted while private, parochial schools
were denigrated (they could not be counted on to force their
students to recite the Pledge like the government-run schools
could).

Students were taught to recite the Pledge with their arms
outstretched, palms up, similar to how Roman citizens were required to hail Caesar. The custom was dropped in the 1940s,
however, when it became apparent that this particular way of
saying the Pledge was eerily similar to the Nazi salute or the
salute of the Italian fascists.

So the Pledge of Allegiance is an oath of allegiance to the
omnipotent, Lincolnian state. Its purpose was never to incul-
cate in schoolchildren the ideals of the American founding fathers, but those of two eccentric, Lincoln-worshipping, utopian
socialists. The War between the States was truly America's
"French Revolution," and Lincoln cultists, in the tradition of
the Bellamy cousins, have worked long and hard to cement the
ideas of that Revolution—especially the supposed imperative of
a "unitary state"—in the minds of American schoolchildren for
generations.

# 18

## The Lincoln Cult
## on Imprisoning War Opponents

It is well known that Abraham Lincoln imprisoned without due process tens of thousands of Northern political dissenters, including many newspaper editors and owners. After the war the U.S. Supreme Court ruled that his actions were illegal because no one—neither Congress nor the president—has the right to suspend the writ of habeas corpus, even in wartime, as long as the civil courts are operating (and they were). But Supreme Court precedents never stand in the way of the Lincoln cult, which believes that the words of one man, Abraham Lincoln, should take precedence over anything else, including the Constitution. A case in point is how certain Lincoln cultists invoked Lincoln's habit of imprisoning his political opponents in order to make *their* case for intimidating, if not imprisoning, opponents of the war in Iraq. If the "sainted" Lincoln did it, they say, then it must be legitimate. Thus, in 2005 and 2006 we observed the spectacle of the website that was established by the "conservative" Heritage Foundation, townhall.com, publishing numerous articles calling for sedition trials for citizens who openly opposed the war in Iraq and invoking the Lincoln precedent of imprisoning *his* war opponents to make their case.[1]

This argument was first on display in a December 23, 2003, *Insight* magazine article by senior editor J. Michael Waller entitled "When Does Politics Become Treason?" "Lincoln's policy was to have treasonous federal lawmakers arrested and tried before military tribunals, and exiled or hanged if convicted." He quoted Lincoln himself as saying, "Congressmen who willfully take actions during wartime that damage morale and undermine the military are saboteurs who should be arrested, exiled or hanged." Lincoln "spoke forcefully of the need to arrest, convict and, if necessary, execute congressmen who by word or deed undermined the war effort," says Waller. Of course, the ever-paranoid Lincoln defined "saboteur" as virtually anyone who disagreed with his policies; that's why he had so many thousands of them imprisoned (and sometimes tortured).

> Modern-day neoconservatives have invoked the Lincoln legend to advocate imprisoning congressional opponents of their imperialistic fantasies.

It is remarkable how Lincoln cultists simply take everything Lincoln said as the Gospel truth, never to be questioned, even if the idea seems absolutely outrageous. To Lincoln, criticizing him or his administration amounted to "warring on the military," which was a treasonous act punishable by death. Clearly, his purpose was to intimidate all of his political opponents in brutal dictatorial fashion. No other American president dared to assert that there should be no political dissent whatsoever—none—during wartime. James Madison even tolerated the noisy New England Federalists' secession movement during the War of 1812. But to Waller these bizarre words should "apply to some lawmakers today," even if said lawmakers insisted that their opposition to the war was "in support of the troops," who they wanted to bring home.

"Exhibit A" of the Lincoln cultists' case for possibly imprisoning congressional war opponents is Ohio congressman Clement L. Vallandigham. Vallandigham was forcefully taken from his Dayton, Ohio, home in the middle of the night by sixty-seven armed federal soldiers, thrown into a military prison without due process, convicted by a kangaroo court military tribunal, and deported.[2]

While a newspaper editor in Ohio and, later, as a congressman, Vallandigham ridiculed the Whig and Republican Party political agenda of protectionism, corporate welfare, and inflationism. He was a states' rights Jeffersonian and a strict constructionist of the Constitution who once said bluntly that he was "inexorably hostile to the Puritan [i.e., New England] domination in religion or morals or literature or politics." He and thousands of other midwesterners were known as "Peace Democrats" who favored working toward a peaceful resolution of the sectional differences that existed. Throughout the Midwest he became known as the "apostle of peace." In Lincoln's mind, advocates for peace and nonviolence could not be tolerated and needed to be deported.

Vallandigham was appalled and outraged at Lincoln's illegal suspension of habeas corpus and his mass arrest of political opponents, as any true Jeffersonian would be. The congressman's alleged "act of treason" was a speech he made on the floor of the U.S. House of Representatives, and later repeated back home in Akron, Ohio, in which he condemned the Lincoln administration's "persistent infractions of the Constitution" and its "high-minded usurpations of power," which were designed as a "deliberate conspiracy to overthrow the present form of Federal-republican government, and to establish a strong centralized government in its stead."[3]

Starting a war without the consent of Congress, Vallandigham said, was the kind of dictatorial act "that would have cost any English sovereign his head at any time within the last two hundred years." Echoing the Declaration of Independence, he railed against the quartering of soldiers in private homes without the consent of the owners; the subversion and imprisonment of the duly elected Maryland government; censorship of the telegraphs; and the confiscation of firearms throughout the border states in clear violation of the Second Amendment.

All of these dictatorial acts were done, said Vallandigham, not to "save the union" but to advance the cause of "national banks . . . and permanent public debt, high tariffs, heavy direct taxation, enormous expenditure, gigantic and stupendous peculation . . . and strong government . . . no more State lines . . . and a consolidated monarchy or vast centralized military despotism." With the exception of "military despotism," these were the exact issues prominent Republicans claimed they elected Abraham Lincoln to promote.

The Lincoln administration argued that Vallandigham's speeches discouraged Ohio boys from enrolling in the military or, worse yet, encouraged desertion from the military, and were therefore treasonous. Essentially, Lincoln claimed his illegal and unconstitutional suspension of habeas corpus was not "treasonous" (to the Constitution) but pointing out his actions in public speeches was.

The Lincoln administration made a big scene of handing Vallandigham over to Confederate authorities in Tennessee in order to create the false impression that political dissenters like the Ohio congressman were spies and traitors. But after having their country invaded, bombed, burned, and plundered for two years by Lincoln's armies, the Confederates wanted nothing to do with a congressman who favored uniting the North and the South. So Vallandigham lived in exile in Canada for the remainder of the war. While there, the Ohio Democratic Party made him its gubernatorial nominee; he lost the election, of course, but it was indeed a heroic act of protest on the part of the Ohio Democrats.

Still, Lincoln was not finished with Vallandigham. The political propaganda arm of the Republican Party, established in 1862, that came to be known as the "Union League," spread incendiary, hateful, and false propaganda about administration opponents, and Vallandigham was certainly the most outspoken, and most prominent, opponent. Historian Frank Klement, who spent his career researching "Copperheads," the defamatory name that Lincoln gave to his Northern political opponents, documented a number of the falsehoods that were spread about Vallandigham in order to "justify" his deportation.[4]

First, the Union League forged a letter that supposedly implicated Vallandigham in the July 1863 New York City draft riots, even though he resided in Ontario, Canada, at the time. Klement proved that this was a forgery, but the story is nevertheless repeated today by members of the Lincoln cult as part of their rewriting of American history.

The Union League forged other documents that claimed it was Vallandigham who persuaded Robert E. Lee to head north into Pennsylvania in June of 1863, leading to the Battle of Gettysburg. The notion that General Lee would base his entire war strategy on the advice of a *Northern* congressman from the same state as Generals Grant and Sherman is preposterous and bizarre, but war sometimes causes normally levelheaded people to suspend their sense of reality. Contemporary historians and writers who continue to spread this false story have no such excuse, however.

Another bizarre lie spread about Vallandigham by the Union League was that he was somehow involved in Confederate John Hunt Morgan's abortive raids into Indiana and Ohio. So the Republican Party attempted to portray Vallandigham as a Wizard-of-Oz-type character who magically controlled the decisions of the Confederate army from Canada, while he simultaneously orchestrated violent attacks *on his own friends and family* in Ohio. Frank Klement proved what a lie it all was.

Interestingly, in his 2003 *Insight* article that seemed to be a clear attempt to intimidate congressional war opponents, Waller wrote that "given the recent controversy about the authenticity of quotations attributed to President Abraham Lincoln, *Insight* went directly to the primary source for the presidential statements about how to deal with congressmen who sabotage the war effort." And what was this trustworthy, primary source? It was an 1863 publication entitled "The Truth from an Honest Man: The Letter of the President," published and distributed by the Union League![5]

> Whenever the government and its private-sector propagandists attempt to deprive Americans of their civil liberties, they inevitably invoke the Lincoln legend as a supposed "justification."

Whenever *anyone* wants to defend the worst kinds of civil liberties abuses, they typically cite Lincoln's precedents, which they always insist are "proof" that the abuses are legitimate and moral. In one case, another Lincoln cultist, neoconservative pundit Michelle Malkin, defended the Roosevelt administration's imprisonment of more than a hundred thousand Japanese Americans during World War II. The prisoners were sent to what FDR himself called "concentration camps," but which

Malkin euphemistically refers to as "relocation centers" in her book *In Defense of Internment.*

Malkin's book is a defense of suspending habeas corpus in the name of waging "the war on terror." In an August 9, 2004, interview about the book on the website Townhall.com, Malkin stated: "Historically, civil rights have often yielded to security in times of crisis. During the Civil War, Abraham Lincoln suspended habeas corpus, which enabled him to detain thousands of rebels and subversives without access to judges." Therefore, she implies, it's okay to do it again today.

This is another patented falsehood—that the tens of thousands of Northern citizens who were imprisoned during the Lincoln administration were "rebels and subversives." The truth is that virtually anyone who opposed administration policies in any way was threatened with imprisonment without due process. This included elected officials, newspaper editors, and thousands of ordinary citizens of the Northern states. Lincoln himself argued that those who simply remained silent and did not publicly support his administration should also be subject to imprisonment. In his own words: "The man who stands by and says nothing when the peril of his Government is discussed cannot be misunderstood. If not hindered, he is sure to help the enemy; much more if he talks ambiguously—talks for his country with 'buts' and 'ifs' and 'ands.' "[6]

Thus, in Lincoln's mind, anyone who did not publicly support his policies was a traitor, susceptible to being prosecuted as such, presumably with the death penalty in some cases. What could be more tyrannical than punishing silence as a crime? This was a

> Lincoln believed in imprisoning citizens who merely remained silent and did not publicly support him and his administration.

common technique of the totalitarian communist countries in the twentieth century, but most Americans would be shocked to learn that the idea was also embraced by Lincoln.

Pro-administration newspaper editors were recruited as a sort of spy network for the Lincoln administration. As Dean Sprague wrote in *Freedom Under Lincoln,* whenever a newspaper editor wanted to cause trouble for a Lincoln critic he would "suggest him as a candidate for Fort Lafayette," the government's gulag for political prisoners in New York harbor.[7]

As word of Lincoln's gulag in New York spread throughout the country, writes Sprague, "the prison cast its shadow over the entire North" and "became a kind of American Bastille, its name on everyone's lips."[8] As such, it was a "weapon" in the hands of the Lincoln administration, used "to establish the fact that the federal government was the greatest power in the nation."

Whenever congressmen requested information about constituents of theirs who were suspected of being imprisoned in Fort Lafayette, Lincoln, whom Sprague describes as "a man of steel," would simply say that it was against the "public interest" to supply such information. This is the kind of "role model" that Lincoln cultists like Malkin routinely cite whenever they advocate yet another watering down of civil liberties in America.

> The only place free speech existed in the North during the war was in the gulags where Lincoln's political prisoners were held.

Lincoln intimidated the Supreme Court by ignoring its rulings, placing federal judges under house arrest, illegally suspending habeas corpus, and even issuing an arrest warrant for the chief justice. He also intimidated Congress by deporting the most outspoken member of the loyal opposition. It wasn't until after the war that the Supreme Court regained the courage and integrity to state the obvious and declare, in *Ex Parte Milligan* (1866), that: "The constitution of the United States is a law for rulers and people, equally in war and peace, and it covers with its shield of protection all classes of men, at all times and under all circumstances. No doctrine involving more pernicious consequences was ever invented by the wit of men that any of its great provisions can be suspended during any of the great exigencies of Government."

In other words, the Supreme Court said that it is precisely in times of national emergencies, such as war, that civil liberties must be defended and protected. If not, then governments will be given an incentive to constantly create crises, or perceptions of crises, as a means of grabbing more and more power. And more governmental power always means less freedom for ordinary citizens.

# 19

## Contra the Lincoln Cult

The Lincoln cult is composed primarily of academics who have chosen careers as, well, cultists. They have their "human capital," in other words, their professional reputations, wrapped up in published articles and books that deify Abraham Lincoln as a Jesus- or Moses-like figure ("Father Abraham") who is routinely described as "the greatest of all Americans" and "redeemer" of the nation, just as Christ was the redeemer of the world. To the cultists, Lincoln is the closest thing to human perfection, a role model for all the ages, nothing less than a *combination* of Jesus and Moses. If one were to watch a Lincoln forum on cable television, one will find much more lavish praise being heaped upon Father Abraham by Lincoln cultists than your typical television preacher will adorn the Lord with in a Sunday morning sermon.

Such rhetoric is rarely beneficial to anyone interested in learning true history, despite the cultists' academic credentials. The cultists tend to be cover-up artists, court historians, gatekeepers, and propagandists more than genuine scholars. Interestingly, in recent years a number of genuinely informative and insightful books and articles on Lincoln have been published by "outsiders"—authors who are not card-carrying members of the Lincoln cult, but simply skilled writers and researchers with inquisitive minds and a thirst for historical knowledge. Unburdened by the mandate to either toe the party line or sacrifice their careers, these writers tend to be much more informative and truthful than the Lincoln cultists are.

One example of this phenomenon is the book *The Great Tax Wars: Lincoln to Wilson—The Fierce Battles Over Money and Power That Transformed the Nation,* by Steven R. Weisman. Weisman is a journalist who wrote about politics, economics, and international affairs for the *New York Times* for more than thirty years. When his book was first published in 2002, he was an editorial writer for the *Times.* The book is a general history of the income tax in America, beginning with Lincoln's income tax in the 1860s. Several sections of the book stand out with regard to the author's analysis of the real Lincoln. In particular, while discussing the secession of the Southern states in 1860–61 Weisman writes:

> South Carolina went first. The state's grievances had been long-standing and not simply focused on slavery. Its major complaint went to the heart of the nation's finances— tariffs. A generation earlier, South Carolina had provoked a states' rights crisis over its doctrine that states could "nullify" or override, the national tariff system. The nullification fight in 1832 was actually a tax revolt. It pitted the state's spokesman, Vice President John C. Calhoun, against President Andrew Jackson. Because tariffs rewarded manufacturers but punished farmers with higher prices on everything they needed—clothing, farm equipment and even essential food products like salts and meats—Calhoun argued that

the tariff system was discriminatory and unconstitutional. Calhoun's antitariff battle was a rebellion against a system seen throughout the South as protecting the producers of the North.[1]

It is clear to Weisman that tariff exploitation was just as important to South Carolina and the rest of the South in 1860 as it was during the nullification fight in 1832.

> The history profession has become so poisoned by political correctness that some of the best research and writing now comes from those who are from outside the profession.

Lincoln cultists are quick to demonize and assassinate the characters of historical figures like Jefferson Davis and John C. Calhoun, while Weisman obviously spent a considerable amount of time educating himself about these men and their political positions and priorities instead. It is refreshing to run across a rare student of Lincoln and the Civil War who is such a transparent truth seeker. Weisman is obviously familiar with Jefferson Davis's first inaugural address, which does not mention the word *slavery* but announces that "our policy is peace, and the freest trade our necessities will permit." He does not describe Davis as a devil but as a hero of the Mexican War, former secretary of war, and a former U.S. senator. He also describes him as "a vigorous exponent of the view that the war was, at its core, not a fight to preserve slavery but a struggle to overthrow an exploitative economic system headquartered in the North."[2] Furthermore, "There was a great deal of evidence to support Davis's view of the South as the nation's stepchild" for "the South had to import two-thirds of its clothing and manufactured goods from outside the region, and southerners paid artificially high prices because of the high

tariffs. . . . The South even had to import food."[3] In short, Weisman has independently arrived at the same conclusions about
the economic sources of the conflict of 1861–1865 as I have. It is
no accident that neither of us is a "professional historian" or a
card-carrying, establishmentarian "Lincoln scholar."

Another "outside" author who shares Weisman's exceptional
historical clarity and hunger for the truth is James Webb, author
of the book *Born Fighting, A History of the Scots-Irish in America.*
Webb is a former U.S. Navy secretary, assistant secretary of
defense, a filmmaker, a highly decorated Vietnam veteran, an
Emmy Award–winning journalist, and the author of several
popular novels.

Webb's focus is on "his people," the Scots-Irish in America.
The Scots-Irish have always been radical individualists: "To
them, joining a group and putting themselves at the mercy of
someone else's collective judgment makes about as much sense
as letting the government take their guns."[4] In the early years of
America they had very little in common with English immigrants who settled in New England—the Puritans and, later, the
"Yankees." Indeed, the American Scots-Irish were mostly
the descendants of people who had been tyrannized for centuries by the British. They became "the dominant culture of
the South," comprised a large portion of the Confederate army,
and were typically yeoman farmers or small merchants who
"had no slaves and actually suffered economic detriment from
the practice" of slavery.[5]

On the subject of Lincoln and his war, Webb asks the
question of why "his people" fought in the way they did. He
quotes the historian Wilbur Cash as noting that Confederate soldiers came from a culture that produced "the most intense individualism the world has seen since the Italian renais-
sance."[6] They never learned to salute as briskly or to become

as obedient as their much more compliant Yankee soldier counterparts.

What all this suggests to Webb is that "It is impossible to believe that such men would have continued to fight against unnatural odds and take casualties beyond the level of virtually any other modern army [70 percent]—simply so that 5 percent of their population who owned slaves could keep them. . . . Something deeper was motivating them, something that appealed to their self-interest as well."[7]

Webb clarifies one particularly telling fact about the average Confederate soldier: He knew that slave owners in Delaware, Maryland, Missouri, and Kentucky were allowed to keep their slaves when the war began. The Lincoln administration's policy was that slave owners could keep their slaves as long as they were loyal to the Union. Indeed, when Fort Sumter was fired upon there were more slave states in the Union than out of it. Consequently, writes Webb, "in virtually every major battle of the Civil War, Confederate soldiers who did not own slaves were fighting against a proportion of Union Army soldiers who had not been asked to give up theirs."[8] This fact spoke volumes to the Confederate soldier about the true causes of the war, and about the Lincoln regime itself.

Webb writes of how the Confederate soldier knew that the Emancipation Proclamation "exempted all the slaves in the North," and in all the areas of the South that were under federal army control at the time. The Southerners understood that the union was voluntary and that the Constitution was on their side: "The Tenth Amendment to the Constitution reserved to the states all rights not specifically granted to the federal

> Former U.S. Navy secretary James Webb has written an important book that exposes the illogic of the Lincoln cult.

government, and in their view the states had thus retained their right to dissolve the federal relationship."[9]

So why *did* the Confederate soldier fight, according to Webb? He fought because "he was provoked, intimidated, and ultimately invaded." His leaders "convinced him that this was a war of independence in the same sense as the Revolutionary War."[10] The "tendency to resist outside aggression was bred deeply into every heart"[11] of every Scots-Irish man, writes Webb. That's why they had to fight. Once again, it takes an outsider to effectively question the "official line" of the Lincoln cult.

In addition to Webb and Weisman, Professor Michael F. Holt, a distinguished historian at the University of Virginia, has challenged cult wisdom in his book *The Fate of Their Country*. Unlike Weisman and Webb, Holt is an academic, but he is not a Lincoln cultist. He is probably the American history profession's top expert on the politics of the antebellum era, having authored the monumental book *The Rise and Fall of the American Whig Party*, and *The Political Crisis of the 1850s*. He's also the coauthor of a textbook entitled *The Civil War and Reconstruction*.

The distinguished University of Virginia historian Michael Holt makes more sense than all of the "Lincoln scholars" combined. Naturally, he is not considered to be one of them.

In *The Fate of Their Country* Professor Holt addresses the question, "What brought about the Civil War?" and concludes the answer is "politics" rather than the North's moral objection to slavery. He correctly points out that slavery was constitutionally secure in 1861; that neither Lincoln nor his party formally opposed *Southern* slavery; that Lincoln supported a constitutional amendment to prohibit the federal government from ever interfering with Southern slavery; and that the issue of slavery in 1860 evolved around its *expansion* into the territories, just as noted throughout this book.

Holt agrees with the thesis of this book, and of *The Real Lincoln*, that the primary reason for the North's (and Lincoln's) opposition to slavery extension was that it would have been a roadblock to the plan of politically and economically dominating the South.

The only moral argument against slavery, one that was articulated by Lincoln, was that stopping the spread of slavery into the territories would supposedly lead to its eventual demise everywhere. Exactly how and why this would occur was never explained, and the theory makes little sense. Slavery was already profitable without expansion into the territories, and besides, it is almost absurd to believe that slavery would have been economical in most of the territories. As Professor Holt concludes, "Modern economic historians have demonstrated that this assumption was false."[12]

Far more Northerners opposed the extension of slavery, writes Holt, because they simply did not want to compete for jobs with slave labor. It was economics, not humanitarianism, that motivated them. In addition, "Many northern whites also wanted to keep slaves out of the West in order to keep blacks out. The North was a pervasively racist society where free blacks suffered social, economic, and political discrimination. . . ."[13] "Bigots, they sought to bar African-American slaves from the West."[14]

> Lincoln and the Republican Party opposed the extension of slavery into the new territories for purely economic and political reasons.

Yet another reason why the North opposed slavery extension was to limit the congressional representation of the Democratic Party. Slaves would increase the population of the territories, which, when they became states, would then have a larger number of congressional representatives. Thus, the real reasons for Republican opposition to slavery extension were purely political and economic, writes Holt.

Why were the Republicans so concerned about blocking the power of the Southern Democrats at any cost—even at the cost of a bloody war? Professor Holt answers this question by quoting the Ohio congressman Joshua R. Giddings: "To give the south the preponderance of political power would be itself a surrender of our tariff, our internal improvements, our distribution of proceeds of public lands. . . . It is the most abominable proposition with which a free people were ever insulted."[15]

Holt contends that Southern politicians were equally responsible for the war as Northern ones were. As he states on the inside cover of his book, "shortsighted politicians [of all parties] . . . used the emotionally charged and largely chimerical [i.e., "wildly fanciful and realistic"] issue of slavery's extension westward to pursue the election of their candidates and settle political scores, all the while inexorably dragging the nation toward disunion."

But if the quest for money and political power was the root cause of the war, as Holt contends, one can hardly hold the South as responsible as the North on moral grounds. It was the North that was attempting to use the powers of the state to plunder the South. The South was acting defensively. The North was the political mugger, whereas the South was the victim of the mugging, with the slaves diabolically used as political pawns.

A fourth writer who dissents from official opinion on the subject of Lincoln is the business historian John Steele Gordon.

Like Weisman, Holt, and Webb, he is an established researcher and writer, but not a member of the Lincoln cult.[16] Consequently, he is free to speak his mind without fear of professional punishment. In his book *Hamilton's Blessing*, about the history of the American public debt, Gordon has this to say about the role of the tariff in precipitating the War between the States:

> A direct confrontation, and, quite possibly, civil war, was avoided only when a new tariff calling for gradually lower rates was adopted [in 1833]. After the [Tariff of Abominations] crisis passed, the tariff continued to decline slowly until the Civil War began for real in 1861. But it remained far higher than required to fund the government's usual revenue needs, and *the tariff, then nearly synonymous with federal taxes, was a prime cause of the Civil War* (emphasis added).[17]

Unlike the Lincoln cultists, Gordon admits that the Republican Party of 1860, led by Lincoln, had an interest in the acquisition of wealth and power, and was not purely a charitable and humanitarian enterprise. And of course, a protectionist tariff was the key ingredient in the acquisition of that power.

The "liberal" writer Michael Lind, formerly an editor of *Harper's* magazine, *The New Yorker,* and the *New Republic,* is another author who has dared to reveal many of the truths about Lincoln and his war that are usually ignored or excused away by Lincoln cultists. Lind is not particularly known as a Lincoln scholar, but in 2005 he came out with a book entitled *What Lincoln Believed: The Values and Convictions of America's Greatest President.* Apparently, Lind's book is acceptable to the gatekeepers because his discussions of unflattering truths about Lincoln are accompanied by enough excuses, rationales, and justifications. And, in the end, Lind concludes that Lincoln was "America's greatest president."

Lind acknowledges that the Lincoln legend has been appropriated from time to time by both the political Left and Right. "The liberal Left, no less than the radical Left, sought to enlist the prestige" of Lincoln to promote its political causes, he writes.[18] Unlike almost all other writers on the subject, Lind emphasizes that Lincoln was devoted to the "Hamiltonian tradition" of economic statism and interventionism. He notes that Lincoln was a longtime Whig, "the party of the educated and economic elites," and that he was, in fact, a "wealthy railroad lawyer" whose "clients included giant corporations, millionaires, real estate speculators, and corporate executives," not a poor backwoods railsplitter. Henry Clay's system of corporate statism, or mercantilism, which involved protectionism, central banking, and corporate welfare, was finally put into place in America by Clay's "disciple Abraham Lincoln" who "adopted Clay's entire . . . program as his own."[19]

Nor does he deny that economics, and not humanitarian issues, dominated Lincoln's political career. Or, that the main opposition to Hamiltonian mercantilism was predominantly based in the South.[20] "If not for the opposition of Southerners in Congress and the White House, many of the government programs that Congress enacted during the Lincoln years, such as national banking, high tariffs, and massive railroad subsidies, would have been enacted decades earlier by the Federalists or the Whigs."[21]

Lind also faults American historians who have "refused to confront the fact of Lincoln's racism candidly."[22] And he does not ignore the truth that Lincoln was not a Christian despite his frequent use of Scripture in his political speeches, acknowledging

that "Despite his lack of Christian faith, Lincoln's oratory is suf-
fused with phrases and images from the King James Bible."[23]

*What Lincoln Believed* also dismisses the absurd notion that
Lincoln was philosophically a Jefffersonian. Lind quotes Lincoln's
longtime law partner, William Herndon, as saying "Mr. Lincoln
hated Thomas Jefferson as a man and as a politician."[24] But
Lincoln was not beyond quoting Jefferson if it served his political ends, just as he was not beyond quoting the Bible if it, too,
would serve his political ends. The reason he made such a big
deal out of the "all men are created equal" line in the Declaration of Independence, for example, was simply to try to win
votes from Jeffersonian Democrats in the border states and the
West who still revered Jefferson.

Lind also acknowledges, rather than covers up, Lincoln's
dreams of "colonization" and of turning America into an all-
white society. The "meteoric rise of Lincoln in national politics"
was greatly enhanced by the fact that he was a "leader of
the Free-Soil movement whose goal was a white West. . . . For
Lincoln, as for most white Free-Soilers, the purpose of prevent-
ing the extension of slavery to the territories was to keep the
West white."[25] Free soilers like Lincoln supported "laws designed
to keep free blacks out of Northern and Western states."[26]

It is possible, after all, to publish truth rather than myth
about Lincoln, as long as one is not a professional historian or a
bona fide "Lincoln scholar."

Yet another example of a book by outsiders who have challenged the Lincoln cult is *Lincoln's Wrath: Fierce Mobs, Brilliant
Scoundrels and a President's Mission to Destroy the Press,* by journalist Jeffrey Manber and historian Neil Dahlstrom. *Lincoln's Wrath*
focuses on the heavy-handed crackdown on freedom of speech
in the Northern states during the Lincoln administration. As
stated in the inside cover: "*Lincoln's Wrath* tells the incredible

story of the overlooked chapter of the Civil War, when the government pressured and physically shut down any Northern newspaper that voiced opposition to the war. The effect was a complete dismantling of the press."[27] "Overlooked" indeed. Newspaper editors in the North who "clung to what many saw as the suddenly out-of-fashion principles of the Constitution," and therefore opposed the Lincoln administration, were shut down by the hundreds by the Lincoln administration, with the full knowledge of the president himself.[28] Any newspaper deemed by Lincoln to be "guilty of being in opposition to the war" was shut down and, in many cases, its printing presses destroyed.[29] Not only that, but editors and owners of opposition newspapers were routinely imprisoned in military prisons without any due process. This behavior would have caused Jefferson, the great champion of free speech, to call for another revolution or war of secession.

## CHALLENGING THE LINCOLN CULT

Weisman, Holt, Webb, Gordon, Lind, and Manber and Dahlstrom have written truths—as opposed to myths and fantasies—about Lincoln and his war. And it is telling that none of them is a bona fide member of the Lincoln cult. As such, they are not in position to be pressured, threatened, or bribed into repeating the party line of the Lincoln cult. This is also true of your author, a professional economist, and of Charles Adams, a tax attorney and historian. It was also true of Edgar Lee Masters (a native of Illinois), Clarence Darrow's law partner who wrote the most critical appraisal of Lincoln to appear in the first century after his death—*Lincoln the Man*.

For generations, Lincoln scholars have been essentially "court historians" who have conspired to deify not only Lincoln, but the presidency in general and, consequently, the American state. All certified members of the Lincoln cult are champions of big government. Liberal Lincoln cultists frequently invoke the holy image of the sixteenth president to promote their favorite causes, from civil rights legislation to the watering down of constitutional restrictions on governmental power. Conservative Lincoln cultists point to Lincoln's brutal, dictatorial militarism and his shredding of civil liberties as they promote *their* favorite cause, foreign policy imperialism. In other words, politics is an important reason why the Lincoln cult so zealously guards the false image of American history that it has created.

> The Lincoln cult is devoted to miseducating Americans about their history.

The deification of Lincoln has always been part of a not-so-hidden agenda to expand the size and scope of the American state far beyond what the founding fathers—especially the Jeffersonians—envisioned. The war itself was a revolution against the Jeffersonian states' rights ideal and the *voluntary* union. That union—the one created by the citizens of the free, independent, and sovereign states when they ratified the Constitution—was *destroyed* in 1865. In its place was put a *coerced* union in which the Southern states, especially, became mere subject provinces rather than sovereigns. Before long, this was true of *all* the states.

American citizens were to be sovereign over their own federal government as members of political communities organized at the state and local levels. With the death of states' rights in 1865 came the death of citizen sovereignty in America.

The Lincoln cult desperately seeks to keep these dark thoughts out of the minds of the American public by creating falsehoods and deceptions about American history. Generations of Americans have been taught the New England version of their country's history, which is filled with lies and fantasies. The idea of federalism, which older generations of scholars recognized as *the central proposition* of the Constitution, has largely been eliminated from American history books. If not eliminated, it is demonized into "states' rights" and associated with slavery and racism.

This, of course, is false. But the Lincoln cult has nevertheless succeeded in miseducating the American public about the most fundamental idea of the Constitution. They are traitors to the American ideal of limited, constitutional, *decentralized* government, and to the personal liberties that system was designed to protect. The Lincoln myths form the ideological cornerstone of the bloated American state, which will never be restored to its proper role until these myths are challenged and overthrown.

# APPENDIX

## What They *Don't* Want You to Read

Many readers of my earlier book, *The Real Lincoln,* have written to ask me, "Why wasn't I taught these things in school?" Good question. "These things," such as Lincoln's suspension of constitutional liberties and his waging war on civilians, are well-documented historical facts that have been available in scholarly publications for generations. But for the most part they have been studiously kept out of the school textbooks. If not, they are usually hidden behind a barrage of excuses and rationales. There are a number of books and publications, however, that allow students of American history to see for themselves what documentation there is for the points made in this book.

### PART I
### What You're Not Supposed to Know
### About Lincoln and His War

#### 2. The Lincoln Myths—Exposed
Publications that expose many of the major Lincoln myths include Jeffrey Hummel's *Emancipating Slaves, Enslaving Free Men,*

which covers most of the important economic and political aspects of the war, as well as some of the military ones. *North Against South: The American Iliad 1848–1877,* by Professor Ludwell Johnson, formerly of William and Mary College, is one of the most insightful and informative books written on the subject in the past century.

An older, classic critique of Lincoln is *Lincoln the Man,* by Edgar Lee Masters. Masters was a native of Chicago, Illinois, and onetime law partner of the infamous attorney Clarence Darrow. He was also a renowned playwright who devoted many years of his life to studying and writing about Lincoln and his war.

Another book is *Forced into Glory: Abraham Lincoln's White Dream,* by Lerone Bennett, Jr., managing editor of *Ebony* magazine. The result of more than a decade of research and writing, and studiously ignored by the Lincoln cult, Bennett's book contains a wealth of facts about Lincoln and his political associates that one would not normally be exposed to in the public schools, universities, and the "mainstream" literature. It is an especially powerful critique, coming from such a distinguished African American author.

*When in the Course of Human Events: Arguing the Case for Southern Secession,* by Charles Adams, is another must-read. Adams is a scholar outside the Lincoln cult who carefully dissects Lincoln's language and actions and presents many important (and well-documented) facts that are usually kept from the public eye by our self-appointed gatekeepers.

A fascinating and fact-filled book is *The Lincoln No One Knows,* by Webb Garrison, who was the author of more than fifty books on Lincoln and the war, and president of McKendree College in Illinois. He describes Lincoln in his concluding chapter as a "self-taught mystic."

An essay by Murray Rothbard entitled "America's Two Just Wars: 1776 and 1861," in John Denson, ed., *The Costs of War: America's Pyrrhic Victories*, is an outstanding analysis that combines history, economics, and philosophy to understand Lincoln and his war. Another important essay in the same volume is Clyde Wilson's "War, Reconstruction, and the End of the Old Republic." Professor Donald Livingston's essay "A Moral Accounting of the Union and the Confederacy" provides a more accurate account of Lincoln's real attitude on the issue of race than is normally provided by the gatekeepers (*Journal of Libertarian Studies*, Spring 2002, pp. 55–105, online at http://www.mises.org/journals/jls/16_2/16_2_4.pdf).

Finally, the "King Lincoln" archives on the website Lew Rockwell.com are worth pursuing. These articles contain links to hundreds of other articles and books that can be indispensable to anyone who is interested in educating himself about the real Lincoln.

### 3. Fake Lincoln Quotes
The first book to consult regarding the validity of quotes attributed to Lincoln is *They Never Said It: A Book of Fake Quotes, Misquotes, and Misleading Attributions,* by Paul F. Boller, Jr., and John George. A classic analysis of Lincoln's use of rhetoric is the late Mel Bradford's book, *A Better Guide Than Reason.* Bradford was perhaps the preeminent Lincoln critic of his time, and a renowned student of rhetoric who taught at the University of Dallas for many years. His book dissects much of Lincoln's political rhetoric in a way that obliterates many of the Lincoln myths.

### 4. The Myth of the Morally Superior "Yankee"
Joanne Pope Melish's excellent book, *Disowning Slavery: Gradual Emancipation and Race in New England, 1780–1860,* was my

primary guide when writing about true Yankee values. An important book about Northern attitudes toward race in the antebellum period is Leon Litwack's *North of Slavery: The Negro in the Free States, 1790–1860*. This book has been largely swept under the rug by the Lincoln cult, but it is a gold mine of historical information. Eugene Berwanger's *The Frontier Against Slavery* also presents a portrayal of race relations in the Northern states that is sharply at odds with the myth of the morally superior Yankee.

C. Vann Woodward's *The Strange Career of Jim Crow* documents how oppressive and discriminatory laws that came to be known as "Jim Crow" laws in the South originated in the Northern states. *Slavery in New York*, edited by Ira Berlin and Leslie M. Harris and published by the New-York Historical Society, catalogues the three-hundred-year history of slavery in that state. *Complicity: How the North Promoted, Prolonged, and Profited from Slavery*, by Anne Farrow, Joel Lang, and Jenifer Frank, is also very revealing and informative.

Finally, a most insightful article is "The Yankee Problem" by Professor Clyde Wilson of the University of South Carolina, online at http://www.LewRockwell.com/wilson/wilson12.html. This was followed by "The Yankee Problem Again" at http://www.LewRockwell.com/wilson/wilson17.html.

### 5. Lincoln's Liberian Connection

The notes from meetings Lincoln held with the free black men in the White House to discuss colonizing Liberia are in *Abraham Lincoln: Speeches and Writings*, which can normally be found at most libraries in America, online, and at all the bookstore chains. The most authoritative book on "colonization" is by P. J. Staudenraus and is entitled *The African Colonization Movement, 1816–1865*. Among the places where Lincoln publicly advocated colonization are in his 1852 eulogy to Henry Clay, his 1854 speech in Peoria, Illinois, an 1857 speech in Springfield, Illinois, and his 1862 message to Congress, all of which are in his published *Speeches and Writings*. In *The Lincoln No One Knows,* Webb Garrison concluded that Lincoln pushed for colonization until the very end of his life.

### 6. An Abolitionist Who Despised Lincoln

Abolitionist Lysander Spooner's letters, and many of his other publications, can be found on the website http://www.lysander spooner.org/bib_new.htm. An excellent book of Spooner's essays, including "No Treason," is *The Lysander Spooner Reader,* edited by George H. Smith. Also relevant is Spooner's book, *The Unconstitutionality of Slavery.*

### 7. The Truth About States' Rights

Forrest McDonald's *States' Rights and the Union: Imperium in Imperio, 1776–1876* is one of the best modern surveys of the American states' rights political tradition. An outstanding and even more contemporary book is *Reclaiming the American Revolution: The Kentucky and Virginia Resolutions and Their Legacy* by William J. Watkins. Published in 2004, this was the first book to be published on the famous Resolves in over one hundred years, thanks to the censorious actions of the "gatekeepers."

James J. Kilpatrick's *The Sovereign States: Notes from a Citizen of Virginia* is in a class all by itself in terms of its scholarship and eloquent writing style by the former nationally syndicated columnist. Professor Clyde Wilson's *From Union to Empire: Essays in the Jeffersonian Tradition* is in the same category. Both of these books are comprehensive treatments of the Jeffersonian, states' rights tradition in America.

*Freedom and Federalism,* by the great "classical" liberal Felix Morley, is also indispensable to understanding the American tradition of federalism or states' rights. The same goes for *Union and Liberty: The Political Philosophy of John C. Calhoun,* edited by Ross M. Lence. *The Essential Calhoun,* edited by Clyde Wilson, is also important, along with *Calhoun and Popular Rule* by Lee Cheek.

### 8. Constitutional Futility

St. George Tucker's *View of the Constitution of the United States* is the best existing source of information on the Jeffersonian view of the Constitution. Tucker's purpose was to "Americanize" *Blackstone's Commentaries* on the law and to explain the Jeffersonian view of the Constitution. A good companion book is *Tyranny Unmasked* by the Virginian John Taylor, which applies the Jeffersonian ideology to the policy and politics of his time (early nineteenth century), especially the tariff issue. Taylor's *New Views of the Constitution* is also a classic.

Gottfried Dietze's book, *America's Political Dilemma: From Limited to Unlimited Democracy,* describes the consequences of abandoning the Jeffersonian states' rights view of the Constitution and adopting the nationalist, Lincolnian view instead. *Secession, State and Liberty,* edited by David Gordon, is a collection of essays about the principles of nullification and secession in the American political tradition.

### 9. Lincoln's Big Lie

When learning about state sovereignty there's no substitute for original sources. Thus, an important reference is *American Historical Documents. The Avalon Project at Yale Law School,* online at http://www.yale.edu/lawweb/avalon. Then there's the old classic by Hamilton, Madison, and Jay, *The Federalist Papers.* The rhetoric of "the whole people" is expertly dealt with in James J.

Kilpatrick's *The Sovereign States,* cited in the last chapter; in Gottfried Dietze's *The American Political Tradition*; and in *Reclaiming the American Revolution* by William J. Watkins, Jr.

## 10. A "Great Crime": The Arrest Warrant for the Chief Justice of the United States

Sources of documentation for Lincoln's arrest warrant for Chief Justice Taney include Frederick S. Calhoun, *The Lawmen: United States Marshals and Their Deputies, 1789–1989*; George W. Brown, *Baltimore and the Nineteenth of April, 1861: A Study of War*; and Benjamin Robbins Curtis, *A Memoir of Benjamin Robbins Curtis.* Legal cases that also document the arrest of other federal judges include *Murphy v. Porter* (1861) and *United States ex re John Murphy v. Andrew Porter, Provost Marshal District of Columbia* (2 Hay. & Haz. 395; 1861). I also recommend Greg Loren Durand, *America's Caesar: The Decline and Fall of Republican Government in the United States of America.* The appendices to this book contain many original documentary sources of Lincolnian tyranny.

The two best books on the topic of Lincoln's unconstitutional and dictatorial behavior are Dean Sprague's *Freedom Under Lincoln* and *Constitutional Problems Under Lincoln* by James Randall, who gatekeeper James McPherson once called "the preeminent Lincoln scholar of the last generation." A more recent edition to this literature is *Lincoln's Wrath: Fierce Mobs, Brilliant Scoundrels and a President's Mission to Destroy the Press* by Jeffrey Manber and Neil Dahlstrom. Historian Frank Klement also included a lengthy discussion of Lincoln's abolition of civil liberties in the Northern states in his book, *Lincoln's Critics. Constitutional Dictatorship,* by Clinton Rossiter, includes an entire chapter on "The Lincoln Dictatorship."

PART II
## Economic Issues You're Supposed to Ignore

### 11. The Origins of the Republican Party
A good reference to the domestic policies of the Lincoln administration is Leonard P. Curry's book, *Blueprint for Modern America: Nonmilitary Legislation of the First Civil War Congress.* A somewhat updated version of this book is Heather Cox Richardson's *The Greatest Nation on the Earth: Republican Economic Policies During the Civil War.* Both authors are proponents of big government and liberal activism, and so are not as critical of this "blizzard of legislation" as they should be. For a more realistic and analytic view of this legislation see Robert B. Ekelund, Jr., and Mark Thornton, *Tariffs, Blockades, and Inflation: The Economics of the Civil War;* and *The Real Lincoln.*

### 12. The Great Railroad Lobbyist
The most informative book on the topic of Lincoln's involvement with railroad corporations is John W. Starr's *Lincoln and the Railroads.* Dee Brown's classic, *Hear That Lonesome Whistle Blow: The Epic Story of the Transcontinental Railroads,* also contains a great deal of information about how the Republican Party cabal profited enormously from engineering the subsidization of the transcontinental railroads. *Lincoln the Man,* by Edgar Lee Masters, includes a discussion of Lincoln's connections to the railroad barons of the mid-nineteenth century.

For the story of how and why subsidies were *not* necessary to build the railroads, see James J. Hill's autobiography, *Highways of Progress,* and Burton Folsom's *The Myth of the Robber Barons.* Also see my book *How Capitalism Saved America: The Untold History of Our Country, from the Pilgrims to the Present.*

## 13. The Great Protectionist

A good source of information on the 1828 "Tariff of Abominations" is Chauncey Boucher, *The Nullification Controversy in
South Carolina.* Another source is W. W. Freehling, *Prelude to
the Civil War: The Nullification Controversy in South Carolina,
1816–1836.*

The story of how Lincoln used his twenty-eight-year reputa-
tion as an ardent protectionist to procure the 1860 Republican
Party nomination is told by Professor Reinhard H. Luthin in
"Abraham Lincoln and the Tariff," *The American Historical Review,* July 1944, pp. 609–629.

Economists Robert A. McGuire and T. Norman Van Cot
argue that the tariff controversy was a much more important
cause of the war than most historians will admit, in "The Confederate Constitution, Tariffs, and the Laffer Relationship,"
*Economic Inquiry,* July 2002, pp. 428–438 (this is one of the top
academic journals in the field of economics).

In *When in the Course of Human Events,* tax historian Charles
Adams devotes several chapters to the role of the tariff in precipitating the war; and the classic history of nineteenth-century
tariff policy is Frank Taussig's *The Tariff History of the United
States.* Robert B. Ekelund, Jr., and Mark Thornton explain the
economics of tariffs in the context of the war as well as anyone
has in their book *Tariffs, Blockades, and Inflation.*

An old classic that includes a very readable analysis of tariffs
in general is Frederick Bastiat's *Selected Essays in Political Economy.* The chapter on international trade in Milton and Rose
Friedman's *Free to Choose* is a good primer on the subject. Another lucid essay is Murray Rothbard, "Protectionism and the
Destruction of Prosperity," online at http://www.mises.org/
rothbard/protectinism.asp. Finally, there's my own article,

"Why Free Trade Works," in the February 1989 issue of *Reader's Digest.*

### 14. The Great Inflationist

Robert Remini's *Andrew Jackson and the Bank War* is a fascinating account of the pitched political battle between Jackson and Nicolas Biddle, president of the Bank of the United States. General references on the history of banking policy in America are Murray Rothbard's *A History of Money and Banking in the United States*; Richard Timberlake's *Monetary Policy of the United States*; and Rothbard's *What Has Government Done to Our Money?* In his book *Emancipating Slaves, Enslaving Free Men,* Jeffrey Hummel has an outstanding and comprehensive discussion of the economics of the "Independent Treasury System" that Lincoln so despised, as well as the banking legislation of the Lincoln administration itself.

Lincoln's publicly stated views on banking policy are found throughout his speeches, especially the one cited in this chapter.

## PART III
## The Politics of the Lincoln Cult

### 15. Making Cannon Fodder

To fully appreciate the arguments for sending our young men and women off to fight wars they don't believe in, one must read *Making Patriots* by Walter Berns. In addition, I strongly recommend Claes Ryn, *America the Virtuous: The Crisis of Democracy and the Quest for Empire.* This book is a scholarly analysis of the mind-set of neoconservatives like Berns who distort history so that it serves their political purpose of transforming America into a militaristic and imperialistic world hegemon (all cloaked in the Lincolnian rhetoric of "virtue" and "civil religion"). Two other books on the rather strange subcult known as the "Straussians" (followers of the late philosopher Leo Strauss), of which Berns is a member, are *Leo Strauss and the Politics of American Empire* by Anne Norton, and *Leo Strauss and the American Right* by Shadia Drury. The chapter on the Straussians in Daniel Flynn's book, *Intellectual Morons,* is also well worth reading.

## 16. Lincolnite Totalitarians

Most Americans who have watched a television documentary on the Civil War featuring prominent Lincoln scholar Eric Foner would probably have a different opinion of him if they read his opposition to the breakup of the Soviet Union in an essay entitled "Lincoln's Lesson" in the February 11, 1991, issue of *The Nation* magazine.

Frank Meyer's warnings about Lincolnian totalitarianism in *National Review* are online at http://www.lincolnmyth.com/without_rhetoric.html. Rothbard's "outing" of William F. Buckley, Jr., as an admitted statist is also online at http://www.lewrockwell.com/rothbard/rothbard6.html.

A good source of information on right-wing totalitarians, like Buckley, who frequently invoke the Lincoln legend to promote their cause is the "Neoconservativism" archives on www.LewRockwell.com. Claes Ryn's *America the Virtuous* is also worth pursuing in this regard.

The biggest reason why Lincoln is always ranked as "our greatest president" by the politically correct, left-wing American history profession is that his political legacy is so supportive of their socialistic, big government agenda. Thus, almost any mainstream book on Lincoln will use his image in some way to advocate even bigger government. One good example of this phenomenon is former New York governor Mario Cuomo's book (with gatekeeper Harold Holzer), *Why Lincoln Matters:*

*Now More Than Ever.* Cuomo and Holzer argue that were Lincoln alive today he would embrace their social democrat/welfare statist political agenda.

### 17. Pledging Allegiance to the Omnipotent Lincolnian State

A good source of information on the origins of the Pledge of Allegiance is John Baer's book, *The Pledge of Allegiance: A Centennial History, 1892–1992.* Since the Pledge was intended by its author to help achieve the kind of "socialist utopia" described in the novel *Looking Backward* by Edward Bellamy, that book is worth pursuing as well. An article that puts the socialist pledge into perspective is Bob Wallace's "The Socialist Pledge of Allegiance," at http://www.LewRockwell.com/wallace/wallace139. html.

### 18. The Lincoln Cult on Imprisoning War Opponents

The December 23, 2003, *Insight* magazine article by Michael Waller entitled "When Does Politics Become Treason?" must be read in order to be believed. It literally suggests punishing dissenting members of Congress's loyal opposition for treason because they voiced doubts about the (second) war in Iraq.

Congressman Vallandigham of Ohio got in trouble with Lincoln because of his speeches advocating a peaceful resolution of the conflict between the North and the South. A good source for those speeches is *The Record of Hon. C. L. Vallandigham: Abolition, the Union, and the Civil War* (Wiggins, MS: Crown Rights Publishers, 1998). Dean Sprague's *Freedom Under Lincoln* contains some fairly detailed descriptions of the "gulags" where Lincoln's political prisoners were held. Frank Klement's book, *Lincoln's Critics: The Copperheads of the North,* is an excellent source of information on Northern opposition to the war in general, and the Vallandigham story in particular.

*Fate of Liberty* by Mark Neely, Jr., is an elaborate excuse for such atrocities, but it does include a great deal of information, such as the revelation that Northern political prisoners were routinely subjected to water torture, among other indecencies.

Michelle Malkin's *In Defense of Internment* was very harshly criticized by defenders of civil liberties (see especially Ilana Mercer, "Internment Chic," http://wnd.com/news/article.asp? ARTICLE_ID=40171). It is worth noting that one of her primary "defenses" was that Lincoln established precedents for imprisoning—without due process—*suspected* "enemies of the state."

## 19. Contra the Lincoln Cult

Steven Weisman, James Webb, and Michael Holt, all outsiders of the Lincoln cult, write expertly and objectively on Lincoln and his time. Weisman's *The Great Tax Wars* is a general history of the U.S. income tax, but contains some exceptionally insightful commentary about the tax policies of the Lincoln regime. Like Weisman's book, James Webb's *Born Fighting* is not about Lincoln or the war per se, but is a history of the Scots-Irish in America. And like Weisman, he makes many wise and well-informed commentaries about these former subjects.

Michael Holt is America's preeminent historian of antebellum politics. He knows a great deal about Lincoln and the war, but that is not considered to be his specialty. I don't consider him, in other words, to be a card-carrying member of the Lincoln cult. His analysis is distinguished from the usual storytelling not only because of Professor Holt's deep knowledge of his subject, but the fact that he is also obviously a keen student of politics, political science, and economics. He is better qualified, in other words, to comment on political economy than are other historians who are less schooled on those subjects but insist on commenting on them regardless. Thus, his book, *The Fate of Their Country,* is a must-read.

Michael Lind's book, *What Lincoln Believed,* generally agrees with all of my arguments about Lincoln the "mercantilist" and political tool of big business, but Lind believes that that was a *good* thing! He mistakenly believes that interventionist policies that benefit particular, politically connected businesses and industries are somehow good for everyone. They are not; they benefit the favored businesses and industries *at the expense* of everyone else. In any event, there are some useful facts in the book. If nothing else, those readers with some education in economics will get a few good laughs.

Finally, *Lincoln's Wrath* by Jeffrey Manber and Neil Dahlstrom is one of the more recent books to reveal some important not-so-pleasant facts about America's sixteenth president, namely, that he had a "mission to destroy the press" in the Northern states—and he succeeded.

# ACKNOWLEDGMENTS

I wish to thank my friend and colleague Lew Rockwell, president of the Mises Institute in Auburn, Alabama, for providing me with a forum for my ideas and writing through both his website, LewRockwell.com, and the scholarly activities of the Institute. All of my fellow academics who work with the Institute have been invaluable sources of ideas and constructive criticism. Another academic "family" that I have benefited from being associated with are all those who work with the Abbeville Institute, founded by Professor Donald Livingston of Emory University.

Both of these institutes, and the people associated with them, are unique in today's academic world in that their objective is the relentless pursuit of truth without any regard whatsoever for political correctness or "acceptability" by the academic "establishment." Indeed, such acceptability would cause them to think they had followed the wrong path.

I also wish to thank my employer, Loyola College in Maryland, for providing an atmosphere of academic freedom in which I can continue to pursue my research and writing without the kinds of interferences that are so commonplace in today's politically correct academic world.

Jed Donahue and Mary Choteborsky of Crown Forum provided me with excellent editorial advice.

Finally, my wife, Stacey, has had great tolerance for my sometimes hermitlike existence with my head in books or in front of a computer for days on end while engaged in my writing. She is always there to support me and my work, for which I am eternally grateful.

# NOTES

## Chapter 1

1. M. E. Bradford, *A Better Guide Than Reason: Federalists and Anti-Federalists* (New Brunswick, NJ: Transaction Publishers, 1994); and Mel Bradford, "The Lincoln Legacy: A Long View," *Modern Age,* Fall 1980.
2. Thomas H. Landess, "Mel Bradford, Old Indian Fighters, and the NEH," http://www.lewrockwell.com/orig4/landess1.html.
3. According to *Webster's College Dictionary,* a cult is a "group that devotes itself to or venerates a person, ideal, fad, etc." or "a religion or sect considered to be false, unorthodox, or extremist."
4. Eric Foner, "Lincoln's Lesson," *The Nation,* February 11, 1991, p. 149.
5. See especially the "King Lincoln" archives on www.LewRockwell.com.

## Chapter 2

1. Robert Johannsen, *Lincoln, the South, and Slavery* (Baton Rouge: Louisiana State University Press, 1990), p. 1.
2. Abraham Lincoln, "Letter to Horace Greely, August 22, 1862," in *Abraham Lincoln: His Speeches and Writings,* ed. Roy Basler (New York: Da Capo Press, 1946), p. 652.
3. Howard Cecil Perkins, *Northern Editorials on Secession* (Gloucester, MA: Peter Smith, 1964), p. 163.

4. Lee Kennett, *Marching Through Georgia: The Story of Soldiers and Civilians During Sherman's Campaign* (New York: HarperCollins, 1995), p. 286.

## Chapter 3

1. Paul F. Boller, Jr., and John George, *They Never Said It: A Book of Fake Quotes, Misquotes, and Misleading Attributions* (New York: Oxford University Press, 1989), p. 77.
2. Ibid., p. 80.
3. Ibid., p. 81.
4. Ibid., p. 82.
5. Alan Guelzo, *Abraham Lincoln: Redeemer President* (New York: Wm B. Eerdmann, 2003).
6. Comment made by Reverend Steve Wilkins at an American history conference attended by the author.
7. Boller and George, *They Never Said It,* p. 84.
8. Ibid., p. 85.
9. Ibid., p. 87.
10. Ibid., p. 82.
11. Ibid., p. 88.

## Chapter 4

1. Clyde Wilson, "The Yankee Problem in America," online at http://www.lewrockwell.com/wilson/wilson12.html, reprinted from the Jan./Feb. 2002 issue of *Southern Partisan* magazine.
2. Joanne Pope Melish, *Disowning Slavery: Gradual Emancipation and Race in New England, 1780–1860* (Ithaca, NY: Cornell University Press, 1998), p. 17.
3. Ibid., p. 32.
4. Ira Berlin and Leslie M. Harris, eds., *Slavery in New York* (New York: New-York Historical Society, 2005), p. 114.
5. Melish, *Disowning Slavery,* p. 285.
6. Ibid., p. 69.
7. Ibid., p. 164.
8. Ibid., p. 64.
9. Ibid., p. 165.
10. Ibid., p. 186.
11. Ibid., p. 199.
12. Ibid. p. 209.
13. Ibid., p. 236.

14. C. Vann Woodward, *The Strange Career of Jim Crow* (Oxford: Oxford University Press, 1955), p. 21.
15. Ibid., p. 20.
16. Ibid., p. 21.
17. Ibid., p. 23.
18. Leon Litwack, *North of Slavery: The Negro in the Free States, 1790–1860* (Chicago: University of Chicago Press, 1961), p. vii.
19. Ibid.
20. Ibid.
21. Berlin and Harris, *Slavery in New York,* p. 4.
22. Anne Farrow, Joel Lang, and Jenifer Frank, *Complicity: How the North Promoted, Prolonged, and Profited from Slavery* (Hartford: The Hartford Courant Company, 2005), inside cover.
23. Ibid., p. xxi.
24. Ibid., p. xxviii.
25. Ibid., p. xxvi.
26. Ibid. p. xxvii.
27. Ibid., p. xxv.

## Chapter 5

1. Lerone Bennett, Jr., *Forced into Glory: Abraham Lincoln's White Dream* (Chicago: Johnson Publishing Co., 2000).
2. Webb Garrison, *The Lincoln No One Knows* (Nashville: Rutledge Hill Press, 1993), p. 186.
3. Abraham Lincoln, "Address on Colonization to a Committee of Colored Men," August 14, 1862, in *Abraham Lincoln: Speeches and Writings, Vol. 2, 1859–1865* (New York: Library of America, 1989), pp. 353–357.
4. Ibid., p. 353.
5. Ibid., p. 354.
6. Henry Mayer, *William Lloyd Garrison and the Abolition of Slavery* (New York: St. Martin's Press, 1998), p. 531.
7. Abraham Lincoln, "Comment on the Dred Scott Decision," June 26, 1857, online at http://www.founding.com/library/body.cfm?id=321&parent=63.

## Chapter 6

1. George Smith, ed., *The Lysander Spooner Reader* (San Francisco: Fox and Wilkes, 1992), p. vii.
2. Ibid., p. viii.

3. Lysander Spooner letter to William Seward, http://www.lysander
   spooner.org/letters_new.htm.
4. Ibid.
5. According to *Webster's Collegiate Dictionary.*
6. Doris Kearns Goodwin, *Team of Rivals* (New York: Simon and
   Schuster, 2005).
7. Ibid., p. 296.
8. Ibid.
9. Spooner letter to Seward.
10. Lysander Spooner letter to Charles Sumner, http://www.lysander
    spooner.org/bib_new.htm.
11. Ibid.
12. Ibid.
13. Smith, *The Lysander Spooner Reader,* p. xvii.
14. Ibid., p. 117.
15. Ibid., p. 118.
16. Ibid.
17. Ibid.
18. Ibid.
19. Ibid., p. 119.
20. Ibid., p. 120.
21. Ibid., p. 121.
22. Ibid., p. xix.

## Chapter 7

1. Dean Sprague, *Freedom Under Lincoln* (Boston: Houghton Mifflin,
   1965), p. 300.
2. "The Kentucky Resolutions of 1798," online at http://www.
   constitution.org/cons/kent1798.htm.
3. James J. Kilpatrick, *The Sovereign States: Notes of a Citizen of Virginia*
   (Washington, DC: H. Regnery & Co., 1957), p. 130.
4. Ibid.
5. Ibid.
6. Ibid., p. 134.
7. Henry Adams, *Documents Relating to New England Federalism* (Boston: Little, Brown & Co., 1905), p. 376.
8. Ibid., p. 338.
9. Virginia Resolution of 1798, online at http://www.constitution.org/
   cons/virg1798.htm.
10. Kilpatrick, *The Sovereign States,* p. 152.

11. Ibid., p. 151.

12. Ibid., p. 152.

13. William C. Wright, *The Secession Movement in the Middle Atlantic States* (Rutheford, NJ: Farleigh Dickinson University Press, 1973).

Chapter 8

1. Gottfried Dietze, *America's Political Dilemma: From Limited to Unlimited Democracy* (Baltimore: Johns Hopkins University Press, 1968), p. 67.

2. Ibid., p. 73.

3. Woodrow Wilson, *Constitutional Government in the United States* (New Brunswick, NJ: Transaction Publishers reprint, 2001), p. 178.

4. Ross Lence, ed. *Union and Liberty: The Political Thought of John C. Calhoun* (Indianapolis: Liberty Fund, 1992), p. 27.

5. St. George Tucker, *View of the Constitution of the United States* (Indianapolis: Liberty Fund, 1999), pp. 1–3.

6. Ibid., p. 24.

7. Ibid., p. 27.

8. Ibid., p. 28.

9. Ibid., p. 112.

10. John Taylor, *Tyranny Unmasked* (Indianapolis: Liberty Fund, 1992), p. 199.

11. Frank Chodorov, *The Income Tax: Root of All Evil* (New York: Devin-Adair, 1963), p. 83.

12. Ludwig von Mises, *Omnipotent Government: The Rise of the Total State and Total War* (San Francisco: Libertarian Press, 1985), p. 268.

13. Felix Morley, *Freedom and Federalism* (Indianapolis: Liberty Fund, 1981), pp. 3–4.

14. The letter is online at http://www.lewrockwell.com/rothbard/rothbard21.html.

15. Adolf Hitler, *Mein Kampf* (New York: Houghton Mifflin, 1998).

16. Ibid., p. 565.

17. Ibid., p. 572.

18. Ibid., p. 566.

19. http://www.yale.edu/lawweb/avalon/presiden/inaug/lincoln1.htm.

20. Hitler, *Mein Kampf,* p. 565.

21. Ibid., p. 575.

22. Ibid.

23. Ibid., p. 578.

24. Edmund Wilson, *Patriotic Gore: Studies in the Literature of the Civil War* (New York: Oxford University Press, 1962), p. xvi.
25. Ibid., p. xviii.

### Chapter 9

1. James J. Kilpatrick, *The Sovereign States: Notes of a Citizen of Virginia* (Washington, DC: H. Regnery & Co., 1957), p. 15.
2. Ralph A. Rossum, *Federalism, the Supreme Court, and the Seventeenth Amendment* (Lanham, MD: Lexington Books, 2001).

### Chapter 10

1. *Murphy v. Porter* (1861) and *United States ex re John Murphy v. Andrew Porter, Provost Marshal District of Columbia* (1861).

### Chapter 11

1. Eugene Berwanger, *The Frontier Against Slavery* (Urbana: University of Illinois Press, 1967), p. 137.
2. Ludwell Johnson, *North Against South: The American Iliad, 1848–1877*, rev. ed. (Columbia, SC: Foundation for American Education, 2003).
3. Joseph Martino, *Science Funding: Politics and Pork Barrel* (New Brunswick, NJ: Transaction Publishers, 1992); Dinesh D'Souza, *Illiberal Education: The Politics of Race and Sex on Campus* (New York: Free Press, 1998), and Tom Bethel, *The Politically Incorrect Guide to Science* (Washington, DC: Regnery Publishing, 2005).
4. James Bovard, *The Farm Fiasco* (Oakland, CA: ICS Press, 1989).
5. Mark Thornton and Robert Ekelund, Jr., *Tariffs, Blockades and Inflation: The Economics of the Civil War* (Lanham, MD: SR Books, 2004).

### Chapter 12

1. David Donald, *Lincoln Reconsidered* (New York: Vintage Books, 1961), pp. 105-106.
2. John W. Starr, Jr., *Lincoln and the Railroads* (Manchester, NH: Ayer Company Publishers, 1981), p. 25.
3. Ibid., p. 58.
4. Ibid., p. 79.
5. Ibid., p. 67.
6. Ibid., p 80.
7. Ibid., p. 152.
8. Dee Brown, *Hear That Lonesome Whistle Blow* (New York: Owl Books, 2001), p. 49.

9. Ibid., p. 31.

10. Ibid., p. 35.

11. Ibid., p. 49.

12. Ibid., p. 58.

13. Ibid., p. 76.

14. Ibid., p. 32.

15. Ibid., p. 64.

## Chapter 13

1. William C. Davis, Letter to the Editor, *North and South Magazine*, March 2004, p. 3.

2. In her 944-page Lincoln biography, *Team of Rivals*, Doris Kearns Goodwin does not even mention the Morrill Tariff of 1861. The only index listing for "Morrill" is for his federal land grant university bill.

3. Chauncey Boucher, *The Nullification Controversy in South Carolina* (New York: Russell and Russell Publishers, 1968), p. 5.

4. Wilson Brown and Jan Hogendorn, *International Economics* (New York: Addison, Wesley and Longman, 1994), p. 121.

5. Clyde Wilson, *The Essential Calhoun* (New Brunswick, NJ: Transaction Publishers, 1992), p. 190.

6. Ibid., p. 192.

7. Milton and Rose Friedman, *Free to Choose: A Personal Statement* (New York: Harcourt, 1980), p. 38.

8. Frank Chodorov, *The Income Tax: Root of All Evil* (New York: Devin-Adair, 1963), p. 36.

9. Frank Klement, *Lincoln's Critics: The Copperheads of the North* (Shippensburg, PA: White Mane Publishing Company, 1999).

10. Jefferson Davis, First Inaugural Address, online at http://www.swcivilwar.com/DavisFirstInaug.html.

11. Roy Basler, ed., *Collected Works of Abraham Lincoln*, vol. 4 (New Brunswick, NJ: Rutgers University Press, 1953), p. 91.

12. Reinhard Luthin, "Lincoln and the Tariff," *American Historical Review* (July 1944), p. 629.

13. Robert A. McGuire and T. Norman Van Cott, "The Confederate Constitution, Tariffs, and the Laffer Relationship," *Economic Inquiry* 40, no. 3 (July 2002), p. 437.

## Chapter 14

1. Michael F. Holt, *The Rise and Fall of the American Whig Party* (New York: Oxford University Prress, 1999), p. 288.
2. Richard Timberlake, *Monetary History of the United States: An Intellectual and Institutional History* (Chicago: University of Chicago Press, 1993), p. 70.
3. Robert Remini, *Andrew Jackson and the Bank War: A Study in the Growth of Presidential Power,* 2nd ed. (New York: W. W. Norton & Co., 1967), p. 19.
4. Timberlake, *Monetary History of the United States,* p. 83.
5. Murray Rothbard, *The Panic of 1819* (New York: Columbia University Press, 1962).
6. Remini, *Andrew Jackson and the Bank War,* p. 144.
7. Ibid., p. 145.
8. Andrew Jackson, "Why the United States Bank was Closed," http://www.lexrex.com/enlightened/writings/bank/jackson.htm.
9. Jefffrey Hummel, *Emancipating Slaves, Enslaving Free Men* (Chicago: Open Court, 1996).
10. David Donald, *Lincoln* (New York: Simon and Schuster, 1996), p. 77.
11. Murray Rothbard, *What Has Government Done to Our Money? Case for a 100 Percent Gold Dollar* (Auburn, AL: Mises Institute, 2005 reprint), p. 78.
12. Murray Rothbard, *A History of Money and Banking in the United States* (Auburn, AL: Mises Institute, 2002), p. 122.
13. *New York Times,* March 9, 1863, cited in Heather Cox Richardson, *The Greatest Nation on the Earth: Republican Economic Policies During the Civil War* (Cambridge, MA: Harvard University Press, 1997), p. 94.
14. Ibid.
15. Ibid.

## Chapter 15

1. Walter Berns, *Making Patriots* (Chicago: University of Chicago Press, 2002), p. 100.
2. Ibid., p. 88.
3. Ibid., p. 87.
4. Ibid., p. 89.
5. Ibid., p. 96.
6. Ibid.

## Chapter 16

1. Edmund Wilson, *Patriotic Gore: Studies in the Literature of the American Civil War* (New York: Oxford University Press, 1962), p. xvi.
2. Frank Meyer, Review of "Lincoln Without Rhetoric," *National Review*, August 24, 1965, online at http://www.lincolnmyth.com/without_rhetoric.html.
3. Ibid.
4. Ibid.
5. Murray Rothbard, "Buckley Revealed," online at http://www.lewrockwell.com/rothbard/rothbard6.html.
6. Ibid.
7. John Haynes and Harvey Klehr, *In Denial: Historians, Communism, and Espionage* (New York: Encounter Books, 2003), p. 40.
8. Eric Foner, "Lincoln's Lesson," editorial, *The Nation*, February 11, 1991.

## Chapter 17

1. John Baer, *The Pledge of Allegiance: A Centennial History, 1892–1992* (Annapolis, MD: Free State Press, 1992).
2. Ibid., p. 3.
3. Claes Ryn, *America the Virtuous: The Crisis of Democracy and the Quest for Empire* (New Brunswick, N.J.: Transaction Publishers, 2003), p. 72.
4. Ibid.
5. Ibid., p. 74.
6. Ludwig von Mises, *Socialism* (Indianapolis: Liberty Fund, 1981), p. 223.

## Chapter 18

1. Horace Cooper, "Not a Suicide Pact," Townhall.com, December 21, 2005; and Ben Shapiro, "Should We Prosecute Sedition?," Townhall.com, February 15, 2006. Heritage sold the website some time in 2005 but the president and editor in chief remained on the job. The site's writers are still ideological clones of the Heritage Foundation staff.
2. Frank Klement, *Lincoln's Critics: The Copperheads of the North* (Shippensburg, PA: White Mane Publishing Company, 1999).
3. *Record of Hon. C. L. Vallandigham* (Jackson, MS: Crown Rights Publishers, 1998).
4. Klement, *Lincoln's Critics*.

5. Michael Waller, "When Does Politics Become Treason?" *Insight,* December 23, 2003.
6. Roy Basler, ed., *The Collected Works of Abraham Lincoln* (New Brunswick, NJ: Rutgers University Press, 1953), vol. 6, p. 264.
7. Dean Sprague, *Freedom Under Lincoln* (Boston: Houghton Mifflin, 1969), p. 29.
8. Ibid., p. 287.

## Chapter 19

1. Steven R. Weisman, *The Great Tax Wars: Lincoln to Wilson—The Fierce Battles Over Money and Power That Transformed the Nation* (New York: Simon and Shuster, 2002), p. 22.
2. Ibid., p. 52.
3. Ibid.
4. James Webb, Born Fighting: *A History of the Scots-Irish in America* (New York: Broadway Books, 2004), p. 9.
5. Ibid., p. 18.
6. Ibid., p. 222.
7. Ibid., p. 223.
8. Ibid.
9. Ibid., p. 224.
10. Ibid., p. 225.
11. Ibid.
12. Michael F. Holt, *The Fate of Their Country* (New York: Hill and Wang, 2005), p. 27.
13. Ibid.
14. Ibid.
15. Ibid., p. 28.
16. Among Gordon's books are *An Empire of Wealth: The Epic History of American Power* (New York: HarperCollins, 2004); *The Great Game: The Emergence of Wall Street as a World Power: 1653–2000* (New York: Scribner, 2000); *The Business of America: Tales from the Marketplace—American Enterprise from the Settling of New England to the Breakup of AT&T* (New York: Walker & Co., 2001); and *A Thread Across the Ocean: The Heroic Story of the Transatlantic Cable* (New York: HarperPerennial, 2003).
17. John Steele Gordon, *Hamilton's Blessing: The Extraordinary Life and Times of our National Debt* (New York: Penguin Books, 1998), p. 56.
18. Michael Lind, *What Lincoln Believed: The Values and Convictions of America's Greatest President* (New York: Doubleday, 2005), p. 9.

19. Ibid., p. 73.
20. Ibid., p. 31.
21. Ibid., p. 18.
22. Ibid., p. 15.
23. Ibid., p. 52.
24. Ibid., p. 102.
25. Ibid., pp. 127, 128.
26. Ibid. p. 130.
27. Jeffrey Manber and Neil Dahlstrom, *Lincoln's Wrath: Fierce Mobs, Brilliant Scoundrels and a President's Mission to Destroy the Press* (Naperville, IL: Sourcebooks, Inc., 2005), inside cover.
28. Ibid., p. 63.
29. Ibid., p. 126.

# INDEX

# Also by Thomas J. DiLorenzo

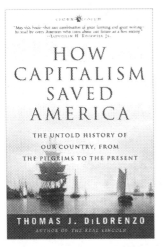

*HOW CAPITALISM SAVED AMERICA* explodes the myths spun by the media, academia, and the rest of the liberal establishment to show how capitalism has made America the most prosperous nation on earth.

HOW CAPITALISM SAVED AMERICA: *The Untold History of Our Country, from the Pilgrims to the Present*
$14.95 ($21.00 Canada) / 978-1-4000-8331-2

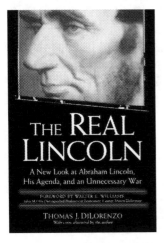

In *THE REAL LINCOLN*, DiLorenzo uncovers a side of Lincoln that you were probably never taught in school—a side that calls into question the very myths that surround him and helps explain the true origins of a bloody, and perhaps unnecessary, war.

THE REAL LINCOLN: *A New Look at Abraham Lincoln, His Agenda, and an Unnecessary War*
$15.95 ($22.95 Canada) / 978-0-7615-2646-9

 THREE RIVERS PRESS • NEW YORK

*Available from Three Rivers Press wherever books are sold.*
*www.crownpublishing.com*

Printed in the United States
by Baker & Taylor Publisher Services